The Otherworld
Music & Song from Irish Tradition

GW00982761

Comhairle Bhéaloideas Éireann

Scríbhinní Béaloidis/Folklore Studies 21

Comhairle Bhéaloideas Éireann 2012
University College Dublin
www.comhairlebheal.ie

Cover image:

View from Inch Beach, County Kerry, 2012.
(National Folklore Collection, UCD)

Design:

Red Dog
www.reddog.ie

Fonts:

Univers
Caslon

978-0-9565628-3-8

Profits from sales of this publication will be
invested in conservation and publication of
the National Folklore Collection, UCD.
www.ucd.ie/irishfolklore

Horseshoe on door,
Claoideach, Gleann na
Ruachtaí, County Kerry, 1946.

Leo Corduff transporting
recording equipment. The
work of the folklore collector
often involved moving
heavy recording equipment.
Here, collector Leo Corduff
negotiates a country lane
near Scotstown, County
Monaghan in 1965.

4

Grateful thanks to the singers, musicians, storytellers and collectors. Thanks also to Anna Bale, Harry Bradshaw, Finbar Boyle, Theresa Buckley, Nicholas Carolan, Rab Cherry, The Coleman Music Centre, Tom Cunningham, Danny Diamond, Marian Deasy, Kelly Fitzgerald, Paddy Glackin, Pat Hedderman, Críostóir MacCárthaigh, Fiachra Mac Gabhann, Fr James McDonagh, Gráinne McGregor, Paul McKeon, Gussie and Eileen MacMahon, Malachy Moran, John Moulden, Terry Moylan, Liam Murphy, Pádraig Ó Cearbhaill, Meaití Joe Shéamuis Ó Fatharta, Seoirse Ó Giolláin, Seán Ó Guairim, Simon O'Leary, Muiris Ó Rócháin, Lisa Shields, Grace Toland, Seosamh Ua Gallchobhair, Paddy Walsh.

We are also grateful to The Arts Council, The National University of Ireland, Na Píobairí Uilleann, Raidió Teilifís Éireann, Irish Traditional Music Archive.

The Otherworld *Music & Song from Irish Tradition*

Electrolux

Puck Fair , Killorglin,
County Kerry, 1952.
Puck Fair is a harvest
celebration. A wild goat
is captured, decorated
and displayed in the town
square for the duration of
the festivities.

Introduction

The notion of compiling a publication of this sort came when we collaborated in the late 1980s on a number of recording projects for Claddagh Records and over the course of a casual conversation we agreed that there did not seem to be many available recordings dealing with music and song associated with the fairies or the Otherworld. Perhaps we might work together on such a project? The seed planted, it took some time to germinate, but now, over twenty years later we have, finally, this publication.

Over those intervening years, many discussions took place regarding the phenomenon of music learned from the fairies and how music and song reflect contact with the 'other side'. For a time *Turas Trasna* [A Journey Across] was adopted as a working name for this project. We thought such a title in some way encapsulated the subject matter and the methodology. The 'journey' travels in and out of the mortal world and the world beyond. It travels throughout Ireland. The compact discs and book are a representative selection from the National Folklore Collection, University College Dublin. Sound recordings represent some of the thousands of voices in this wide-ranging and extraordinarily rich resource. The examples, whether sound recording, manuscript or photograph, come from different parts of Ireland. Of the thirty-two counties on the island of Ireland only counties Longford, Offaly and Derry are not represented here, which is not to suggest that these three counties are somehow lacking in folklore dealing with the Otherworld.

There are islanders and city dwellers represented here. There are farmers, teachers, housewives, Travellers, students - just a few are professional musicians. There are stories and songs in Irish and in English. Of course, it should be borne in mind that here we have selected just a tiny sample of the large volume of material contained in the National Folklore Collection that deals with the aspects of the Otherworld.

Even into the twenty-first century traditional music and song remain a vital part of the cultural fabric in contemporary Ireland. The rich heritage of music, song and related lore is frequently referenced by the Irish public, and often the Irish state, as central to the nation's identity. While music, dance and song reflect a key aspect of our inherited traditions they do not exist alone, or in isolation from other aspects of lore and tradition but are an integral part of the community from which they come. Social context, associated lore and the dynamic process of related song, story, custom and belief are vital parts of the presentation and performance of music and song. The function of narrative lore in the transmission of traditional music and song remains central - context and history are established - songs are named, composers or revered players acknowledged, if only sometimes, in the tune titles. In talk and stories about songs or tunes a shared sense of inclusion can be subtly added to with each telling, with each piece of knowledge shared. A session of music and song is made even more intimate by the re-telling of a yarn associated with a certain musician or by some speculation about where a tune came from, how it was transmitted or who played it in a certain fashion. Community, identity and continuity are supported and celebrated in the singing of songs and the playing of tunes. In this sense, narrative lore and human interaction serve a critical role in sustaining and enriching the social process of music making.

A belief in the Otherworld is a prominent feature in the lore of Ireland. Tales, legends and lore associated with the world of the *sí*, the *púca*, ghosts, revenants and mermaids are central to the fabric of that lore. Preternatural or supernatural beings and events are commonplace and occur in different forms. Characters, tunes, motifs, themes, place names and verses continually serve to remind us that there is a very real sense of the existence of the Otherworld.

Belief in otherworldly existence or events is not confined to any one part of the country or to any particular level in society. At the time of going to print sixteen of the thirty-eight contributors featured in the sound recordings were living. The earliest recording dates from the early 1920s while some of the material was recorded in recent years. This is detailed in the Recording Sources listing on page 151. Of the forty recordings presented on the two compact discs which accompany this book there are seventeen songs - six of which are in English and eleven in Irish. There are also seventeen recorded pieces of music – five of which are lilted. One set of jigs is whistled, eight pieces are played on the fiddle, one played on the tin whistle, one played on the wooden flute and one on the uilleann pipes. The preponderance of the fiddle here reflects its position as arguably the most commonly played instrument in Irish music.

The subject matter in the songs and some of the tune titles reflect the wide range of belief associated with aspects of the Otherworld. The Otherworld here is taken to mean a domain relating to the preternatural, an alternative realm parallel to or sometimes beyond human earthly existence. The music, song and lore in this publication touch on many aspects of such belief - from prophetic warnings of punishment in the afterlife for unnamed sins to seemingly chance encounters with fairies or otherworldly creatures, prophecy, benign meetings with the fairies and the transference of special or unusual powers, tales of violent revenge for acts of cruelty, revenants reveal themselves to former lovers, musicians set astray at night with marked improvement in their playing skills, innocence betrayed, and justice served as a result of ghostly visions, a nocturnal murderess, fabulous underground realms, fairy abduction, humourous views of otherworldly creatures, death messengers, dreams as portents of disaster, music transmitted from the afterlife, vaguely erotic encounters between fairy women and poets, aspects of the man-made and physical landscape explained through association with the non-mortal realms, references to ancient deities, moralistic warnings against nocturnal rambling and drinking, fearful encounters with hooved creatures, spellbinding otherworldly music, treasure and gifts bestowed by the fairies, a sea creature married to a mortal, water as a protective boundary, sporting engagements among the fairies, a *leipreachán* outwits a mortal, terrifying sounds explained, mysterious hunger pangs and heightened otherworld activity at certain key times of the year. The grotesque, the marvellous, the cautionary and the humourous are here. The role or function of the tale or song can vary from simple entertainment to an attempt to grapple with metaphysical issues and profound questions.

Perhaps it is fundamental to the human condition that we imagine the possibility of something beyond our temporal sphere? It could be argued that there is a sense that we confront the unknowable through the invention of an other parallel existence. Some form of a relationship with the supernatural is a universal trait. The material presented here reflects some of the circumstances, hopes, anxieties, fears and beliefs of Irish people. At times, the lore can be seen as an attempt to articulate the incomprehensible and the apparent cruelty and injustice of the natural world. A faith in the existence of something beyond the everyday is common to almost all of humanity. While this underlies religious and spiritual belief it may also support the possibility of the existence of the supernatural. What the rich material presented here reflects is a peculiarly Irish angle on universal themes. Some of the songs and stories are known in other countries and cultures - for instance the story associated with the tune known as 'Bá Phroclaise' [The Bruckless Drowning] is a south-Donegal version of an internationally-recorded migratory legend sometimes known as 'The Ship-Sinking Witch'. There are a number of narrative lyric songs or ballads here that are known and sung in other traditions - versions of 'The Cruel Mother', here called 'Down By the Green Roadside-um', and 'Willie O' among them. Such songs migrated to Ireland through ballad sheets or chapbooks or perhaps were carried in the minds and memories of settlers, travellers and migratory workers. Others were composed in this country – for example 'Amhrán an Frag' [The Song of the Frog]. Some of the songs deal with the local – named landmarks and individuals serve to establish a sense of place and assumed familiarity. Examples of lore of places and place names indicative of musical and otherworldly music activity abound – for example, Lisadell, Cathair an Phíobaire or Rathmore. The following example illustrates some of the layers of legend and belief associated with music, the Otherworld and landscape.

In the case of the various megalithic standing stones and stone-circles that are called 'The Piper's Stone(s)', the sound that the wind made as it blew around these sharp-angled monuments was thought to be the music of fairy pipers. Occasionally, though, human pipers were in question. For instance, Carraig an Phíobaire 'The Piper's Rock', in the parish of Menlo, co. Galway, was named for the music of a fairy piper. (Donnelly 2001, 23)

In the same parish however, Cloch na bPíobairí, 'the Pipers' Stone' was so named because it was where pipers sat and played during hurling matches. Otherworld or unworldly music is often heard at particular points in the landscape such as boundaries, bridges and standing stones.

The fairy world exists alongside the world of mortals. The *sí,* as they are often known in Irish, are generally invisible to mortals but exist very much in the manner of humans as they occupy themselves in terms of amusement and work in the manner of mortal beings. Place names and sometimes even the physical landscape support the belief in the closeness of the fairy world to the world of humankind. The *sí* are reputed to live in *líosanna* or raths or cairns. Most of these, incidently, are man-made features common in the Irish landscape. The fact that sometimes these mounds were burial places and may have long enjoyed a supposed connection with the ancient world enhances the sense of mystery and reverence that can be associated with them. Fairies were both feared and respected. People generally believed it unlucky to call fairies by their name and consequently appelations such as *na daoine maithe* [the good people], *na daoine uaisle* [the gentry] or *bunadh na gcnoc* [the people of the hills] were used out of respect and fear. Individual otherworld or fairy personages such as Fionnbhearra, Clíona or Áine were treated with awe and are still associated with particular places or realms. Otherworld activity is especially prominent at particular times of year such as May and November marking the liminal time between one season and the next. Fairies and otherworld beings become involved in human activity and vice versa. May Eve and All Hallows Eve were particularly believed to be times associated with increased preternatural activity. In the light of documented folk tradition in Ireland, belief in the fairy world, in another 'world' or sphere of existence parallel to that of mortals was extremely strong. The belief in a world largely invisible to mortals but nonetheless believed to run parallel to human

existence, is arguably one of the ways people try to rationalise what appears to be inexplicable to them. Calamity at sea or untimely death might be explained by curses and fairy abduction. A curious natural phenomenon such as a whirlwind can be blamed on the *slua sí* [fairy host] passing. Personal loss and an implicit sense of grief are found in the tale of the mermaid abandoning her mortal children to return to her original home in the ocean in the song from Donegal, 'An Mhaighdean Mhara'.

Much of the material here deals with the fantastic and unusual and can be understood to represent a contrast to the monotony and drudgery of physical labour and day-to-day chores. Mysterious appearances or disappearances challenge boredom and encourage imaginative engagement. The ability to temporarily leave, or be taken from, this mortal world and enter another, often fabulous, realm is fantastical. Sensual imagery, feasting, wealth and unasked for gifts can suddenly materialise and just as quickly disappear. The banal can become wondrous in story and song. Everyday things can be invested with mystery and otherworldly attributes: from common weeds to the largest mountain; from the wind blowing in a certain direction to cloud formations and from the behaviour of domestic animals to chance encounters.

Very often these encounters were unsolicited and fortuitous. Sometimes benign, these meetings were not always so - to cross paths with the fearsome Petticoat Loose was not something to be desired. To inadvertently step on the *fóidín mearbhaill,* an enchanted piece of ground or grass, would result in the unwary traveller being set astray. Some of the human protagonists here exist on the edge of society - wandering musicians, wise women, *cailleachaí,* rakes and night ramblers. There can sometimes be an implicit cautionary message in some of the songs or stories. Thoughtlessness, selfishness and meanness on the part of the fishermen in 'Bá Phroclaise' [The Bruckless Drowning] result in them drawing down a fatal curse. We find also a macabre fascination with murder, the dead, and with graves in songs like 'The Heart's Delight' and 'Cruel Willie'. There are tensions between mortals and the fairy world, between the living and the dead, the realms of good and evil. Metaphorically this can be represented by day and night, light and dark. A sense of liminality of being between time is conveyed. The revenant leaves before daybreak. Cock-crow signals the time that evil spirits must withdraw. Sometimes in the Otherworld humans experience a loss of power. In the song 'Seachrán Sí' [Set Astray by the Fairies] normality is turned on its head in the temporary other form of existence experienced in the fairy realm.

Some tales communicate desirable or undesirable social behaviour and may, for example, caution against covetousness and greed while recommending generosity and helpfulness. A well-attested tale is the story of the man who has a hump and when the mortal completes the fairies' rhyme *Dé Luan, Dé Máirt* [Monday, Tuesday] with *Dé Céadaoin* [Wednesday] his hump disappears. When another man, who has heard the story, appears and adds yet another day to the rhyme *Déardaoin* [Thursday], the rhythmic flow is lost and then the fairies give the second man an additional hump. A version of this tale has been published in *Síscéalta ó Thír Chonaill: Fairy Legends from Donegal* (Ó hEochaidh *et al.* 1977) and a music transcription of the song appears in *Irish Music and Song* (Joyce 1903). A man out late at night distilling *poitín* is approached by a mysterious piper who conveys a sense of threat. Holy water is used to defeat the menacing piper. Such recourse to elemental protection is not uncommon and we encounter also the power of metal against spells or otherworldly abduction. Societal disapproval of those contravening accepted moral behaviour or breaching or challenging convention can result in the accusation of an otherworld association. Sometimes an authority figure – a priest in two of the stories here - confronts such an individual. Excesses are challenged. More prosaically, a community's need for diversion and entertainment can be witnessed in the shame expressed by the man with only one tune. If recourse had to be found in supernatural intervention then so be it!

The Otherworld can have threatening and undesirable aspects. Exceptionally it can be treated in a lighter tone. The fact that it is used in a light-hearted fashion indicates a sense of acceptance and familiarity. It is a human trait to sometimes joke about what frightens us, the purpose being to dissipate tension and fear. The jaunty mock-heroism in songs like 'Amhrán an Phúca' [The Song of the Pooka] contrasts with the 'reality' of belief in the *púca* as malevolent and evil. This is something akin to whistling past the graveyard.

The links between mortal and immortal, between 'here' and 'there' in tales, legends, songs and tunes share common characteristics. Throughout the oral material a fear of, and respect for, a realm beyond the mortal is reflected. One of the most frequently documented tales is the legend telling of a transfer of music, or of the gift of music, from an otherworld being to a mortal with the result that the mortal musician plays music of exceptional quality. This legend reflects the important function of music and song in Ireland. It also underlines the high esteem in which talented musicians and singers are held. The accounts are arguably a means by which the gift of exceptional talent in the realm of music and song may be explained within Irish oral tradition. The music historian and writer, Caoimhín Mac Aoidh, has a humourous twist on the international legend of a musician encountering the devil at a cross roads. He tells of a county Derry fiddler named Mooney who, driven from his home by a cantankerous and music-hating wife, forlornly tramps the roads and at midnight chances upon a cowled figure at a crossroads. The stranger greets Mooney and noticing his fiddle asks if he might play a tune. Mooney is greatly impressed with the stranger's music and demands to know his name. Dramatically throwing back his hood the horned head of the Devil is revealed. Instead of cowering in terror as might be expected Mooney extends his hand saying, 'Meet your relation, I'm married to your sister'.

Some tune titles suggest an otherworldly connection. These include 'The Fairy Reel', 'An Mhaighdean Mhara' [The Mermaid], 'The Lilting Banshee' or 'Port na bPúcaí' [The Tune of the Fairies]. Certain tunes have otherworld links because of the associated lore. Examples of such tunes are 'An Rógaire Dubh' [The Black Rogue], 'Tiúin an Phíobaire Sí' [The Tune of the Fairy Piper] and 'Ceann Boirne' [Black

Head]. Legends associated with the music of exceptionally talented musicians such as the fiddle players Michael Coleman and Néillidh Boyle imply otherworldly intervention as a possible explanation for their celebrated musical prowess. The collector Francis O'Neill included numerous references to, and accounts of, the importance and role of the good people and their world in music. He suggested that inspiration was commonly believed to derive from the fairies or other supernatural agencies. He stated, for example, that the itinerant harper Carolan's composition 'Bridget Cruise' was inspired by Carolan's proximity to a fairy dwelling:

> Near his father's house was a rath, in the interior of which one of the Fairy Queens or "good people" was believed by the country people to hold her court. This rath or fort was the scene of many a boyish pastime with his youthful companions; and after he became blind, he used to prevail on some of this family or neighbours to lead him to it, where he would remain for hours together, stretched listlessly before the sun. He was often observed to start up suddenly, as if in a fit of ecstasy, occasioned as it was firmly believed, by the preternatural sights which he witnessed, In one of these raptures he called hastily on his companions, to lead him home, and when he reached it, he sat down immediately to his harp and in a little time played and sung the air and words of a sweet song addressed to Bridget Cruise, the object of his earliest and tenderest attachment. So sudden and so captivating was it, that it was confidently attributed to fairy inspiration. (O'Neill 1913,71)

Carolan flourished in the early eighteenth century and one of his reputedly earliest compositions was entitled 'Sí Bheag, Sí Mhór' and took its name from two fairy raths near to Lough Scur in county Leitrim where the harper was in residence in the home of one of his patrons, Squire George Reynolds.

The strange, lasting effect of otherworld music has been documented in other accounts. Michael Coffey, Riverview, Bonmahon, Co. Waterford, for example, wrote as follows on November 4th 1947.

In the townland of Williamstown in the parish of Stradbally once lived Michael Coffey who owned a farm. This farm contained a wood in the centre of which was a very large rock. From time to time stories were told by people – that they had heard strange music when passing near the wood at night and that the music seemed to come from the direction of the rock. My father – Michael Coffey – often heard these tales but paid no heed to them. One night, however, as he was retiring home he was charmed by the most beautiful music from, as he thought, a violin and coming from the direction of the rock in the wood about a quarter of a mile from his home. He remained for a while listening when suddenly the music became very mournful and there seemed to be crying mingling with the tune. My father became nervous remembering the accounts he had heard from neighbours about the strange music heard in the wood and he hurried away from the place and continued his way home. Some years afterwards, in the year 1897, the wood was sold and cut down. Shortly after that my father went to the place to quarry stones to build houses. He blasted the rock and when it fell to pieces he was surprised to find in the middle of the hard rock two tallow candles as yellow as gold. He took them home to see if they would light and they burned beautifully giving a peculiar blue flame. The music was never afterwards heard and the rock remains to this day. I have a distinct remembrance of these happenings and I saw the candles burning and remarked on their strange light. I was about ten years old at the time. My father died on the 19th May 1919, aged 72 years. (NFC 1710:405-406)

Changelings frequently feature in narrative lore. A changeling is thought to be a fairy being left in place of the mortal who has been taken away by the fairies. The identification of a changeling by mortals often comes about by means of the performance of music. If the person suspected of being a changeling plays unusually fine music, this is taken as proof that he or she is, in fact, a changeling. To this end, pipes, or another instrument, were left beside the changeling and when wondrous music was heard coming from the room, the mortals believed that a changeling was playing. There is a story told by Martin Talty, Miltown Malbay, Co. Clare to Harry Bradshaw in 1985, of Garrett Barry, a famous piper, that he was left to mind a one-year-old child while the child's parents were away. Garrett thought that the child was asleep and started to play his pipes. The child spoke from the cradle to Garrett, saying: 'You're good but I've heard better'. When the child's parents came home they struggled to believe the story, but the child was said to have died a short time later.

The song tradition in Irish and English tells of encounters with the Otherworld, of the dead and of revenants. It tells of ghosts, mermaids and inhabitants of otherworld dwellings. The Queen of the Fairy Rath – 'Banríon na Bruíona' features in the song 'An Aill Eidhneach' [The Ivy-covered Rock] and Fionnbhearra, the king of the fairy host in Cnoc Meá, near Tuam, Co. Galway, is mentioned in 'Amhrán na Siógaí' [The Song of the Fairies]. The song 'Cailín Deas Crúite na mBó' [The Pretty Girl Milking the Cows] introduces a group of songs that were believed to be cursed and understood to bring misfortune to those who broke the rules of tradition and sang these songs. Without the associated lore, the song loses its otherworld connections. Betrayed or murdered lovers might return or appear after death and in some songs the chill of a ghostly return is evident, as in 'Cruel Willie'.

These examples of music and song of the Otherworld are part of the more general body of Irish traditional music and song. They might arguably be regarded as representing a tradition which is found well beyond the island of Ireland. A legend, which might be entitled 'The Musician in the Cave' has been documented in Ireland, Scotland, England and Wales and describes a musician, normally a piper, who enters a cave, playing an instrument. He is heard playing for a while and then the sound of music disappears. Subsequently ghostly music is heard coming from the cave, sometimes on special occasions. (MacNeill 1962, 668). Legends and stories abound linking the playing of music and otherwordly creatures. In 1966, the writer Frances Collinson observed:

> Shetland, like the Hebrides, has its fairy tunes, there called 'Trow' tunes. They are said, like those of the Hebrides, to have been heard issuing from the fairy mounds or in other ways heard from the playing of the 'trows,' and to have been picked up and remembered by the passing wayfarer. (Collinson 1966, 259)

In Norway we find reference to 'troll tuning' for the traditional Hardanger fiddle, this scordatura tuning is associated with music thought to have been learned from the devil, so-called 'fanitullen' tunes. Sweden too has its otherworldly inspired fiddle tuning called 'näckastamning'. Fiddle playing water spirits in Sweden called 'Näcken' are reputed to draw people to their doom in water or to inspire dancing which could often result in death or madness. Such beliefs are widespread.

An original source or creator of most of the material is unknown. It might be said that this anonymous origin lends authenticity to it as folk tradition. It is also probable that over time, the name of the original maker or source has been forgotten. In some cases, however, a composer of a tune or a song-maker is named. Junior Crehan, for instance, is the composer of 'The Lútharadán's Jig', while 'The Moving Clouds' is attributed to Néillidh Boyle. We know also the composers of some of the songs in Irish contained in this publication. It should not be assumed that all the composers or song-makers were literate. Regardless of an identified or unidentified original source, the songs, music and associated narrative offer a window on a particularly striking aspect of Irish lore. Not every tune or song with accompanying lore has survived, been recorded or collected. Some songs and tunes will survive in the mouths and the playing of new generations. Others cease to be spoken of, played or sung and may eventually be forgotten.

Context and society change but traces of the power of some of the beliefs referred to in this material remain even today. Are there many in Ireland who would consciously cut down a lone bush or desecrate a 'gentle' place? Belief in the banshee persists. Many still afford respect to the fairies and ambivalence as to the existence or otherwise of 'the good people' is not uncommon. One can still come across a deliberate vagueness or elusive responses in relation to questions concerning otherworld beliefs. This is exemplified in the title of a paper by the collector Tom Munnelly, who contributed so much to this publication 'They're there all the same'. Certain places retain a 'creepy' or 'scary' reputation. Fortune tellers and psychics appear on television. Healers are visited. Divination, prophecy and superstition are still to be found. Lotto players invest faith in certain numbers. Wells are still visited for cures. Teenagers enthusiastically consume books and television series relating to vampires. Human nature is such that strong religious faith or its absence can still allow for other forms of belief. Remnants of an older, pre-Christian, faith are still to be encountered. Children still celebrate Samhain. Bonfires continue to be lit on certain days of the year and other observances, particularly in relation to calendar customs, still continue.

While the music, song and lore are absolutely central to this publication, the labour of those who documented this body of work deserves special recognition. Their dedication to the recording and transcription of the material contained here reflects the respect and, indeed, love the various collectors shared not just for that material but also for the singers of songs, the tellers of tales and the makers of music.

Ríonach uí Ógáin & Tom Sherlock

Blacksmith, Waterville, 1947,
County Kerry. The blacksmith's
forge was sometimes located
at crossroads. In addition to its
everyday work function, the
forge could serve as a meeting
place or centre of gossip and fun
on inclement days.

Collectors, Recordings, Transcriptions, Accounts and Images

The recordings were made for the most part as part of ongoing fieldwork for the Irish Folklore Commission or its successor the National Folklore Collection, University College Dublin. Their formats include acetate disc, cassette, reel-to-reel tape, digital audio tape, minidisc and memory card. The context of recording varies a great deal as recordings were made outdoors in a field, in a car, or indoors in houses, for example. All recordings were remastered by Harry Bradshaw.

We have particular reason to be indebted to Tom Munnelly, a Dublin-born song collector and indefatigable champion of traditional songs and singers. Tom Munnelly who recorded almost all the English-language songs on these cds, was employed by University College Dublin. Tom's love of the song tradition in Ireland is reflected in the thousands of songs he recorded during his more than thirty-year period as collector before his death in 2007. He catalogued thousands of songs according to various international ballad classification systems. Although Tom often commented on the quality of the songs, their singers and their versions of songs, he remained open to the fluid and changing nature of traditional song.

Other collectors include Ciarán Bairéad, Caoimhín Ó Danachair, Leo Corduff Seán Ó hEochaidh and Michael J. Murphy all of whom were officers with the Irish Folklore Commission. Examples of narrative excerpts have been included from the audio and manuscript archives of the National Folklore Collection. Without the efforts and fieldwork of collectors in recording and documenting these traditions, the National Folklore Collection would not be the remarkable resource it undoubtedly is. The voice of the people speaks to us through the work of these collectors. The imagination and creativity that gave rise to the stories songs and music here echo still for us and, indeed, that imaginative engagement with the Otherworld continues.

Comhairle Bhéaloideas Éireann/ The Folklore of Ireland Council is particularly grateful to RTÉ and especially to Malachy Moran for permission to include tracks from its radio archive. Recording officers with Radio Éireann such as Ciarán Mac Mathúna and Paddy Glackin are represented in this publication. More recent fieldwork undertaken in the last few years has augmented some of the older recordings. The recent recordings serve to remind us that musical expression continues to flourish in Ireland and that the documenting of this tradition is ongoing and contemporary. While that tradition draws inspiration from the past, thanks in no small part to archives and bodies like the National Folklore Collection, it also moves forward into whatever the future will bring it.

Fairy Bush, Mill Street,
Antrim. Fairy bushes are
generally associated with rural
locations. Here is one in a town.

Down by the Green Roadside–um

sung by Mickey Connors

For as I was going down by my
daddy's garden,
All alone and alone, alone-ee,
I seen three babes and they playing a ball,
Down by the green road side-um.

There was one of them was dressed in blue,
All alone and alone, alone-ee,
And the other of them was naked 'twas born,
And it's down by the green road side-um.

Oh daddy, dear when I was yours,
All alone and alone, alone-ee,
You dressed me up in neither coarse nor fine,
And it's down by the green road side-um.

Oh babe, oh babe you know right well,
All alone and alone, alone-ee,
For which shall I go to, heaven or hell?
And it's down by the green road side-um.

You'll be seven years a stone in a bridge,
All alone and alone, alone-ee,
You'll be seven more a miaowing cat,
And it's down by the green road side-um.

You'll be seven more a *sceach* in a gap,
All alone and alone, alone-ee,
You'll be seven more a curl-tailed rat,
And it's down by the green road side-um.

You'll be seven more a pigeon in white,
All alone and alone, alone-ee,
And up to heaven you will take your flight,
And it's down by the green road side-um.

- That's all I know of it.

The Otherworld *Music & Song from Irish Tradition*

Burial ground for
unbaptised children
with Ogham stone,
Valentia, County
Kerry, 1946.

A sinister encounter lies at the heart of this version of the song more usually known as 'The Cruel Mother', sung here by Mickey Connors. The song usually tells of a woman, often unmarried, who gives birth to and murders her children. Following their burial, she sees children at play and in an apparent sense of guilt, tells how she would dress them and take care of them. It is an international ballad which is also known as 'Down by the Green Wood Sidey-O'. Curiously, one of the most popular of children's songs in Ireland, 'Weila, Weila, Waila' appears to be related. 'The Cruel Mother' includes accounts of murder and, sometimes, of incest. For this reason, singers could be reluctant to sing the song. Mickey Connors' version differs from the more commonly sung versions in that one of the three babes addresses the subject of the song as 'Father' and foretells the punishment his soul will undergo. The final stanzas here are generally associated with the song 'The Well Below the Valley' which is also known as 'The Maid and the Palmer'. In 'The Well Below the Valley' a woman has had a number of partners and given birth to children by different fathers. She is given various punishments to atone for her 'sins'.

The singer, Mickey Connors, was a Traveller and this recording was made at a campsite in Tullow, County Carlow, on 22nd February, 1972. Mickey told Tom Munnelly that he learned the song from his father. Tom also recorded a version of the song from Bernie Lawrence, a settled Traveller in 1973, with the title 'Down by the Green Wood Sidey-O'. The air of the song is a version of one of the more common melodies to which 'Barbara Allen' is sung.

Tom Munnelly (1944-2007) made the largest known collection of traditional Irish song sung in English. Originally from Dublin, Tom became a professional collector of traditional song and lore. He moved to County Clare in 1977 and made sound recordings and created a photographic record of songs, singers and of related lore for the following thirty years. In the course of his career, he collected throughout Ireland from singers, musicians and storytellers.

The Otherworld *Music & Song from Irish Tradition*

Tom Munnelly

His collected work is now part of the National Folklore Collection. Tom transcribed the songs and lore he collected and also created an electronic index of English-language and macaronic song contained in the first two thousand volumes of the National Folklore Collection. He lectured and published widely, primarily on the ballad and song tradition in Ireland and also on aspects of collecting and of oral tradition.

———

There is a big house below Kinvara and it is known as the residence of Baron de Bastro, a French gentleman. There is a cross near the house, namely 'geata bán' [white gate]. In olden times people used pass from midnight until two o'clock a.m. and some people used be killed and more chased back.

There was a man from the district who lived in Newquay. One night his wife was ill, and he had to go into Kinvara for a nurse. When he reached the cross a ghost in the shape of a woman appeared before him. She halted him and she asked him where was he going, and he told her. He said to her: 'Don't murder me or you will take the life of three', and she let him pass and he said to her: 'I will come again at the same time tomorrow night.'

The man went and told the parish priest. The priest told him to bring holy water and make a round circle with his foot and sprinkle holy water around it. The priest gave him a cock and he let go the cock at the cross. The bird flew back to the priest and let three crows.

The priest set out on his journey. When he reached the cross, he asked the ghost what was troubling her. She told him and he said: 'I will forgive them.'

'I killed my father, I killed my mother, I killed a child that was not baptised.'

The priest said: 'I will forgive you. Have you anything else troubling you?' 'I killed myself,' said the ghost. 'I won't forgive you,' said the priest. 'But you must leave this spot.' He sent her to a place in Carrigaholt, County Clare. The calmest day that ever came, the sea is very wild around the spot.

Told by William Moran, Ballinamanton, Gort, County Galway to his daughter, Ann Moran, Convent School, Gort, 1937-1938. (NFCS 50:68-69)

The Schools' Manuscripts Collection of 1937 – 1939 was an impressive and far-sighted initiative undertaken by the then fledgling Irish Folklore Commission to encourage primary school teachers to ask their pupils to record stories, tales and lore from their immediate families and neighbours. A vast body of material was collected by means of the scheme in which around a hundred thousand pupils aged between eleven and fourteen gathered local folklore for the Irish Folklore Commission. Following a selection by teachers from the original school copybooks in which the pupils wrote essays, certain pupils were asked to transcribe from the copybooks into larger notebooks for binding in the archive of the Commission.

The narrative above is set on the borders of south Galway and north Clare. Like the song above, recorded by Tom Munnelly from Mickey Connors, the story Moran told his daughter is rich in supernatural motifs. He establishes that the setting for his story takes place at a crossroads close to the residence of an exotically named foreigner. Crossroads were often thought to be places of ghostly or diabolical association and were sometimes the place of the sacrificial burial of animals. The 'witching hour' of midnight is mentioned. Dangerous and sinister events are stated to happen at this place. Moran introduces a female ghost, a priest, blessed water, a magical circle, a cock that, significantly, crows a total of three times. Among powers attributed to the cock was the power to banish evil spirits. The priest challenges the ghostly form and a tale of murder and infanticide unfolds.

Jig Learnt off the Fairies

played on the fiddle by Mickey Doherty.

This is a jig that has been learnt off the fairies in Teelin. I heard my uncle Mickey saying that there was a man learnt it off the fairies. He was a Mickey Mac Connell. I heard him saying that before he died. That's about thirty years ago. So he used to play it himself on the fiddle.

Legends and accounts of learning or acquiring a particular tune from the fairies are well-attested to in Irish oral tradition.

Mickey 'Simey' Doherty (1894 – 1970) came from a Donegal family of travelling musicians and tinsmiths. Mickey was one of eight siblings who were highly-regarded as fiddle players. Mickey and his brother John were the best known. Mickey married when he was nineteen years old and he, and his wife Mary, had five sons and four daughters. While the children attended school, Mickey and Mary settled in Glenfinn. He travelled around and crafted household utensils and bought and sold fiddles, in addition to making them. Mickey was proud of his musical inheritance and regularly played for dancers in local houses. He often visited the Irish-speaking district, Na Cruacha, at the foot of the Blue Stack Mountains. Fairy belief and lore were elements of life at the time and Mickey bears witness to this here.

This slip jig was one of several tunes recorded on acetate disc from Mickey Doherty for the Irish Folklore Commission by Caoimhín Ó Danachair and Seán Ó hEochaidh in a house in Na Cruacha in January 1949. The tune was published in 1990 by Comhairle Bhéaloideas Éireann on the publication *The Gravel Walks: The Fiddle Music of Mickey Doherty* which contains about a hundred minutes of the three hours of music recorded on that occasion.

The Otherworld Music & Song from Irish Tradition

Mickey Doherty

Caoimhín Ó Danachair

Seán Ó hEochaidh was appointed full-time collector with the Irish Folklore Commission in 1935, when he was twenty-two years old, and he worked in this capacity until his retirement in 1983. A native of Teileann, County Donegal he documented the stories, songs and traditions throughout his county and collected material, in Irish for the most part, from over a thousand people. He lectured and published a great deal.

Originally from Athea, County Limerick, Caoimhín Ó Danachair first began his work with the Irish Folklore Commission in 1940. His primary interest was in ethnology, a subject on which he published and lectured throughout his career. He also spearheaded the establishment of the photographic archive now in the National Folklore Collection. He travelled around Ireland and frequently made sound recordings with some of the full-time collectors such as Seán Ó hEochaidh and Seosamh Ó Dálaigh.

Bhí fear ann fadó agus bhí fidil aige agus ní raibh sé in ann a bhualadh ar an bhfidil ach an dá phort. Cé ar bith é, phós duine muintearach dó agus hiarradh eisean chuig an mbainis agus é an fhidil a thabhairt leis le a bheith a bualadh ceoil dóibh. By dad, bhí an fear bocht in an-riocht, níor mhaith leis a n-eiteach agus bhí leisce air nuair nach raibh sé in ann a bhualadh ar an bhfidil ach an dá phort cé (go té) an chaoi a gcaitheadh sé an oíche, oíche fhada go maidin a bhualadh an dá phort chéanna i gcónaí.

Ar deireadh agus ar siar rinne sé misneach imeacht, bhuail sé an fhidil faoina ascaill agus bhuail amach. Ní raibh sé i bhfad ón teach nuair a casadh fear dó. Bheannaigh an fear dó agus bheannaigh seisean dósan.

'Bhfuil aon dochar fiarfaí,' arsa an fear, 'cá bhfuil tú ag gabháil?'

'Níl,' ar seisean, 'chuig bainis atá mé ag gabháil, agus tá mo sháith drochmhisnigh orm ag gabháil ann.'

'Níl a fhios agam cén t-ábhar drochmhisnigh atá agat,' arsa an fear, ' faoi a bheith a gabháil chuig bainis. Sílimse dá mbeinn in d'áit go mbeinn i mbród an domhain.'

'A, ní drochmhisneach,' ar seisean, 'uilig atá orm, ach tá mé iarraithe acu le haghaidh ceoil agus níl mé in ann a bhualadh ar an bhfidil ach an dá phort agus beidh a bhfuil sa teach ag magadh fúm féin agus faoin dá phort.'

'Feicim anois,' arsa an fear, 'go cén ábhar drochmhisnigh atá agat, ach ná déanadh sin imní ar bith dhuit. Seinn an fhidil domsa go fóill.'

Thóig sé an fhidil amach as an gcása agus thug dó í. Thug seisean cúpla stráca di agus thug ar ais dó í.

'Anois,' ar seisean, 'níl ábhar drochmhisnigh ar bith agat, níl aon phort sa domhan nach féidir leat a bhualadh ar an bhfidil sin anois in mo dhiaidhse.'

Chuir sé an fhidil isteach sa gcása aríst agus d'imigh leis go ndeachaigh go teach na bainise. Fuair sé isteach agus thoisigh air a bualadh ceoil agus a leithéid de cheol níor mhothaigh siad ariamh le a fheabhas agus a bhí sé. Ní raibh aon phort a dtiocfadh leat cuimhniú air nach raibh sé in ann a bhualadh. Ní raibh léamh ná insean scéalaíochta air ina fhidiléirí as sin amach.

Cathaoir Ó Dochartaigh (68), Ceathrú Thaidhg, Béal an Átha, Contae Mhaigh Eo a thug do Mícheál Ó Sírín, 17.3.1951. (CBÉ 1207:43-45)

Long ago there was a man who had a fiddle and he could only play two tunes on the fiddle. A relation of his married, and he was invited to the wedding and asked to bring the fiddle along to play. By dad, the poor man was in a dreadful state as he did not want to refuse and yet was reluctant as he could only play two tunes and wondered how he would pass the night, a long night until morning, playing the same two tunes all the time.

The Otherworld Music & Song from Irish Tradition

At long last, he plucked up his courage and decided to go. He put the fiddle under his arm and set off. He hadn't gone far from the house when he met a man. The man greeted him and he greeted the man.

'Is it any harm to ask,' said the man, 'where you are going?'

'No,' he said, 'I am going to a wedding and I am very disheartened about going.'

'I don't know why you are disheartened,' said the man, 'about going to a wedding. I think if I were in your shoes I would be very excited.'

'Oh, it's not entirely lack of courage,' he said, ' but I have been invited to play music and I can only play two tunes on the fiddle and everyone there will laugh at me and at the two tunes.'

'I understand now,' said the man, 'why you are disheartened, but don't worry. Give me the fiddle a while.'

He took the fiddle out of the case and gave it to him. He gave it a few strokes and handed it back to him.

'Now,' he said, ' you have no reason to be discouraged, there isn't a tune in the world that you can't play on that fiddle now that I have played it.'

He put the fiddle back in the case again and went off until he arrived at the wedding house. He went in and began playing music and they never heard such music, it was so good. There wasn't a tune you could think of that he couldn't play. He was renowned as a fiddle player from that day on.

Told by Cathaoir Ó Dochartaigh (68), Ceathrú Thaidhg, Ballina, County Mayo to Mícheál Ó Sírín, 17.3.1951. (NFC 1207: 43-45)

County Mayo on Ireland's north-west coast is where this version of a commonly recorded story was collected sixty years ago. A fiddle player, on his way to play music at a wedding, is granted marvellous powers following a chance meeting on the road with a mysterious man. This is an example of a benign encounter with an otherworldly creature and one way of rationalising why extraordinary artistic talent occasionally emerges.

Seán Ó hEochaidh

Bá Phrochlaise [The Bruckless Drowning]

lilted by Cití Seáin Ní Chuinneagáin

Legends bearing testament to sympathetic magic occur in Irish and international oral narrative. In some instances, if a certain woman is refused assistance or alms, those who have refused are cursed and may pay the ultimate price for their lack of charity. The story of the ship-sinking witch is a migratory legend, a story that is hundreds of years old. Versions have been collected in Iceland, Norway, Sweden and elsewhere. Migratory legends have often become attached to certain historical events or characters, in this instance a drowning tragedy that happened in the early nineteenth century at Bruckless bay in south Donegal.

The well-documented tragedy known as 'The Great Bruckless Drowning' occurred on February 8th, 1813. A large herring-fishing fleet was operating in Bruckless at the time. The men came from Donegal town, Inver, Ardara, Teileann and St John's Point. As they set out this particular evening, the sea was calm and the weather good. However, a storm arose and following the disaster, it was estimated that between 300 and 500 fishermen were lost.

The tragedy is said to have been caused by an old woman, Biddy Devenney, who cursed the fishermen and their boat for their refusal to give her a supply of fish.

She used to visit the boats every morning regularly, to ask for her share of herrings. For a time, the fishermen were happy to give her a share until her requirements began to appear excessive. The fishermen then decided that they would no longer agree to her demands and refused to give her the herrings.

The old woman vowed she would seek revenge and ordered a local girl to bring a basin of water. The old woman then set a coppan or wooden bowl floating on the top and asked the girl to watch the water. When the girl observed the water becoming agitated the old woman began her cursing and following the woman's third query about the state of the water, the reply was that the water was in a rage and the bowl turned upside down. Following the drowning, Biddy was never seen again. An account of the event is documented in the study of the Irish dialect of Teileann published in the book *Gaeilge Theilinn* written by Heinrich Wagner in 1959.

The legend and the piece of music named after the drowning were recorded by the piper and collector Séamus Ennis for Radio Éireann in 1949 from Peadar Ó Beirn (Peadar Johnny Johndie) of Bealach Bhun Glas, An Charraig. The translation below was made by Seosamh Ua Gallchobhair. Peadar and his sister Máire claimed that a piper could be heard playing the tune while the disaster was happening.

In the year 1813 when the Teileann fishermen were fishing in wee boats before they got big boats or anything else from the English Government or from any other source there was only the sail and the four oars and the poor creatures had to be everywhere while a man had the power and fitness to pull an oar. And there was no place around near home, where there was anything going, but they would have to be there to earn a pound.

But one year, as I have said already, they had to go over to Bruckless and there is a dirty bay there. But one night as the story goes, as they were getting ready to go to sea, a wee old woman came – she must have been a witch; she came round the place and the fishermen started blackguarding and making devilment on her and one fellow grabbed a spiny dogfish or something and threw it at her. But he didn't know whom he was haranguing. Anyway, one man from the fleet asked them to let her be for they did not know who she was. When she seen that he had more sense than the rest, she went over to him. 'Well, you there, don't you go to sea tonight,' says she, 'and you'll not be any the worse off in the morning.' But there were four or five members of his family fishing with him in their own boat

The Otherworld Music & Song from Irish Tradition

and they were making fun and teasing their father for giving in to an old woman of that kind because of the ranting but it made no difference. When he put any doubt in it, he said he would not go to sea and some of his family went out in other boats against his bidding.

But when they had their nets shot, the night changed and before long there was a severe 'Way of Sorrow and Lamentations' in that place. The night changed and it got so bad that the first crews that had hauled their nets were being drowned as they reached the land and it seems it was so when all was over and finished, a great slaughter had happened and after the drowning, the widows left were numbered in many hundreds.

Anyway, it seems that there was someone whose attention was taken away from the disaster – he heard somebody – a musical instrument – most likely a piper it was believed – there was a musical instrument on the shore and it was believed to be a piper because it is a piper that follows that kind of slaughter and witchcraft and all sort of capers of that kind. But anyway, there was somebody who had the tune with him.

Cití Seáin Ní Chuinneagáin carries a rich store of music and dance, which she acquired from her family and neighbours in Cruachlann, Teileann where she was born on 24 October, 1919. Her grandmother, Bidí John Chitín was a great lilter, and through Bidí, Cití is related to the fine fiddle players - 'The Cassidy's - John, Paddy, Frank and their cousin, Con. Cití spent a great deal of time visiting the musical household of Máire, Peadar and Conall Ó Beirn. She first heard 'Bá Phrochlaise' from Peadar. Cití is a singer, lilter and dancer. Although now over ninety years of age, Cití retains the same lively, youthful energy she has had since she was a young girl.

Tá Cití Seáin Ní Chuinneagáin ar maos sa traidisiún ceoil agus rince a fuair sí óna muintir féin agus óna comharsana i gCruachlann, Teileann, an áit ar rugadh í ar an 24ú Deireadh Fómhair, 1919. Bhí a seanmháthair, Bidí John Chitín ina portaire iontach maith, agus trí Bhidí bhí Cití

Houses in south-west Donegal, 1946.

gaolta leis na scothfhidléirí 'Na Caisidigh,' John, Paddy, Frank agus a gcolceathrar, Con. Chaith Cití tréimhsí fada in éineacht le Máire Ní Bheirn agus a deartháireacha, Peadar agus Conall, teach ceolmhar, oscailte eile sa cheantar. Ba ó Pheadar a mhothaigh sí 'Bá Phrochlaise' ar dtús. Is amhránaí agus rinceoir í Cití freisin. Cé go bhfuil sí os cionn deich mbliana agus ceithre scór, tá an fuinneamh ceoil céanna aici agus a bhí aici nuair a bhí sí ina girseach.

Fear óg a bhí ag iascach in éindí le foireann as an mbaile a raibh sé ann agus féibrí cén easaontas a d'éirigh, cuireadh as an mbád é agus ní raibh ag a mháthair ach é agus nuair a tháinig sé abhaile agus nuair d'inis sé dhi gur cuireadh as an mbád é, bhuail fearg agus darta mhire í agus chroch sí pota ar an tine agus nuair a thosaigh sé a fiuchadh dúirt sí leis an mac báisín beag maide bhí aici chur síos sa bpota ag snámh ar bharr an uisce bhí ann agus chuir sí tine mhór faoin bpota ansin le go mbeadh oibriú tréan ar an uisce nuair a bheadh sé a fiuchadh. Dúirt

sí leis an mac a bheith a faire an photá agus chuaigh sí féin idir dhá ghiall an dorais ina seasamh agus bhí an mac ag inseacht di cén chaoi raibh an báisín agus an pota ag obair, ach faoi dheireadh is faoi dhó dúirt an mac go raibh an báisín iontaithe is a bhéal faoi sa bpota.

'Tá na gnaithe déanta anois,' a deir sí, agus bhí an bád ar cuireadh an mac aisti, bhí sí báite sa bpointe sin.

I gcontae Mhaigh Eo in áit eicínt a d'éirigh an chúis sin, níl a fhios agam baileach cén áit. M'athair a chloisinn ag cur síos air.

Colm Ó Caodháin, Glinsce, Carna, Contae na Gaillimhe a thug do Shéamus Mac Aonghusa, 1944-1945. (CBÉ 1281: 407-408)

A young man was fishing with a local crew and whatever disagreement arose, he was sent off the boat and he was an only child and when he came home and told his mother that he had been sent off the boat she became angry and flew into a rage and she hung the pot on the fire and when it began to boil she said to her son to place a small wooden bowl of hers floating on the water in the pot and she lit a large fire under the pot then so that the water would become quite agitated when it boiled. She told her son to keep watch over the pot and she placed herself standing between the two jambs of the door and the son was telling her how the basin and the pot were faring until finally the son said that the basin was turned, face down in the pot.

'That job is complete now,' she said, and the boat from which her son had been sent off, it was drowned at this point.

This happened in County Mayo somewhere, I'm not sure where. I heard my father tell of it.

Told by Colm Ó Caodháin, Glinsce, Carna, County Galway to Séamus Ennis, 1944-1945. (CBÉ 1281: 407-408)

Cití Seáin Ní
Chuinneagáin

The Otherworld Music & Song from Irish Tradition

The story on the theme of the ship sinking
witch above is from Colm Ó Caodháin, who
was one of the great sources of song and lore
for Séamus Ennis. Ennis was perhaps the most
widely known of the collectors with the Irish
Folklore Commission. Colm reminds us that his
story is located in Mayo, a neighbouring county
to Galway. It involves an only child and an
intemperate and vengeful mother who wilfully
causes harm and destruction. The necessity of
standing between the door jambs is in order to
occupy a liminal position of 'neither here nor
there' and indicates power which is conferred
by being outside the realm of the day-to-day
and associated with the 'in between'. The
concept is well-attested to in Irish and in
international folk tradition.

Fairy Bush, County
Clare, 1972.

The Heart's Delight

sung by Austin Flanagan

There was a lord lived in this town,
He was a lord of high renown,
He had one daughter a beauty bright,
And the name he called her was his
heart's delight.

There did many a lord to court her came,
But none of them could her favour gain,
Till at length came a lord of a high degree,
And above them all, she fancied he.

One night as she was for bed bound,
Just stripped and ready to lay down,
She heard a dead and a dismal sound,
Saying: 'Untie those bonds love,
they are fast bound.'

Her father's steed was the first she knew,
Her mother's mantle and safeguard too.
Saying: 'Here's a token to your beauty bright,
For your father loves you to come to-night.'

She dressed herself in rich attire,
She rode away with her heart's delight,
And when he got her up behind him,
He rode far swifter than any wind.

An olive handkerchief she did pull out,
And around his head she did fast bound.
She kissed his cold lips, those words did say:
'*Mo mhíle stór*, you're as cold as clay.'

So when she came to her father's hall,
Her father was the first one she did call,
Saying: 'Father, father, did you send for me,
By such a messenger?' naming he.

The father knowing that this young man
was dead,
And many a green leaf growing o'er his head,
He clasped his hands and he cried full sore,
Whilst the young man's darling cried more
and more.

Generally this song concludes with a verse that proclaims that although the young man has been dead for twelve months, the unity of lovers' bonds transcends death. The lines 'For once their hands and their hearts they give/ They never can recall' are decipherable on the recording. As the collector, Tom Munnelly, commented: 'Slightly incomplete text. The verse where her father then sends her to a house fifty miles away is missing.'

Tom Munnelly made his first recording of 'The Heart's Delight', an international ballad, in Blacklion, County Cavan in 1972. He had a special fondness for this particular song and spent a number of years actively seeking it out. He often quoted the first two lines of the song and then asked singers if they had ever heard the song. 'The Heart's Delight' is also known as 'The Holland Handkerchief', 'The Suffolk Miracle' and 'The Sweetheart's Delight'. The song is quite old and was in print in Britain by the late seventeenth century. 'The Heart's Delight' is the ballad analogue to the international folktale 'The Dead Bridegroom Carries off his Bride'. For additional information and provenance in Ireland see also Uí Ógáin/O'Connor 1983.

Tom Munnelly summarised the song in his catalogue in the following manner:

> Lord's daughter has many rich lovers but chooses a man of high (low) degree. One night her lover visits her to bring her back to her father's house. She mounts behind him. When he says his head is sore she gives him a handkerchief to wrap his head. He leaves her to stable the horse. She goes in to her father who is terrified when he hears her story, for he knows the young man is dead. She and her uncle go to the burying place wherein the corpse is dug up to reveal the Holland handkerchief.

The Otherworld Music & Song from Irish Tradition

Austin Flanagan explained to Tom that the handkerchief was wound around the man's head when he was buried. He also said he heard old people singing the song. Tom noted that part of this song was contained in a manuscript songbook written by Austin and his brother Michael *c.* 1925. Tom said he had made a copy of this. Austin learned the song as a child from a neighbour, John Devitt.

Austin Flanagan was a farmer and was about fifty years of age when Tom Munnelly made this recording in Austin's home on 30th July, 1974. Austin, his brother Michael and sister Katie lived together in Doolin and Austin was the youngest of the three with Katie being the eldest. Irish was spoken a good deal in the area when the Flanagans were young. Austin died in 1995.

Both Austin and Michael were keen followers of the sport of hurling and were known to travel to Thurles and Limerick to matches. Other siblings John, May, Delia, Paddy and Martin went to live in Australia. This appears to be the only occasion on which Tom made recordings of Austin and he recorded seven songs from him. During the same recording session, Tom recorded ten items, including some lilting, from Austin's older brother Michael who was renowned for his mouth music. Michael's repertoire included a number of songs with historical and political themes.

Before this particular recording session took place, Tom had visited the Flanagan brothers in mid-July in search of songs. They said they would be happy to be recorded by him the next rainy day. Tom's diary entry for this recording session reads:

Crosses at Kilmore, County Wexford, 1946. A new cross was added to the pile when a funeral passed by.

Once again I have been lucky in my work. Today was a terribly wet day, so I returned to the Flanagan brothers in Doolin. Got some very good songs and lilting in a long recording session. After a great deal of persuasion, I was able to get them to part with a very tatty old copybook in which they had a lot of songs written.

———————

I mBaile an Mhuilinn a thit sé sin amach agus is é an méid a chuala-sa do, bhí ceo agus cúthalán ar an dtaobh thuaidh de Bhaile an Mhuilinn agus gheall an buachaill seo, abair leat féin, go raghadh sé a triall uirthi agus go bpósfaí iad. Maraíodh an buachaill ar an slí ach go háirithe agus tháinig sé ag triall ar an gcailín agus é marbh agus a chapall agus a shrian agus iallait aige agus chuaigh sí in airde ar an gcapall chuige agus gan aon fhios aici go raibh sé marbh. Nuair a bhíodar ag gabháil thar Abha Bhaile an Mhuilinn:

'Spor ar an gcois,' ar sise.

'Spor ar an gcois' ar seisean 'agus gan an chos ann, agus gan de bhrí insa chois ach mar bheadh cúr na habhann.'

Sin é an uair a thuig sí í féin agus chaith sí í féin anuas den gcapall agus bhain sí an tigh amach chomh maith agus d'fhéad sí. Sin a gcualasa dho san.

Séamas Ó Beoláin (82), Baile an Liaigh, Fionn Trá, Contae Chiarraí, a d'inis do Sheosamh Ó Dálaigh, 15.5.1940. (CBÉ 701:39-40)

This happened in Milltown and from what I heard, there was mist and, 'cúthalán' north of Milltown and this lad promised, I suppose, that he would go and fetch her and they would marry. The boy was killed, however, along the way and he came to fetch the girl, although he was dead and he brought his horse, reins and saddle with him and she got up on the horse behind him, unaware that he was dead. As they were crossing Milltown River:

'Spur with your foot,' she said.

'Spur with your foot' he said 'but there's no foot there, and no more strength in the foot than the froth of the river.'

It was then she understood and she threw herself off the horse and went home as quickly as she could. That's all I heard about it.

Told by Séamas Ó Beoláin (82), Baile an Liaigh, Fionn Trá, County Kerry to Seosamh Ó Dálaigh, 15.5.1940. (NFC 701:39-40)

Here we have an example of 'The Dead Bridegroom carries off his Bride' collected by Seosamh Ó Dálaigh or Joe Daly, who was a fulltime folklore collector from 1936-1951. Seosamh spent most of his collecting career in his native Kerry. This was recorded from Séamus Ó Beoláin from just west of the town of Dingle in Kerry. Séamus was born in 1858. It is no accident that having established the location of the story we are told that a fog descends prior to the unexplained death of the main character and ghostly encounters ensue. Folk belief in Ireland has it that supernatural creatures have an aversion to water and to metal. A widespread belief had it that otherworldly spirits could not cross running water.

The Coleman Brothers' Strange Experience

told by P.J. Duffy

We're standing here now beside that field where Michael Coleman and his brother Jim were supposed to have this strange experience way at the early ears of the century. But, they were supposed to end up in a beautiful garden with lush grass and cattle grazing away in the fields. They kept on walking and it opened up into a vast landscape … They sat down on a stone and started playing music and the music sounded, the most beautiful music that ever they heard came from that fiddle that night and it sounded and sounded and echoed across these beautiful plains. Just as sudden as it came about, the whole thing faded away. There was a noticeable improvement in the music as a result of this.

P.J. Duffy, Killavil, County Sligo here narrates a story to radio producer, Harry Bradshaw, that adds an air of mystery to the legend that surrounds the reputation of the exceptionally talented fiddle player Michael Coleman. Jim Coleman, a brother of Michael's is reputed to have been the source of the story. The well-known Sligo fiddle player, Fred Finn, retold it to P.J. Duffy. P.J. located the field where the strange experience is said to have occurred and pointed out that it contained an historical fort said to be two thousand years old. Local legend has it that Jim Coleman was carrying a fiddle which had been tuned by a travelling musician on this particular night. P.J. also recounted how strange things had happened to other people in a field at the other side of the field where there was a fairy path and people were set astray at night there.

Many oral accounts tell of musical talent being transferred by mysterious, otherworldly means. In a relatively small area of south County Sligo a distinctive fiddle playing style developed in the mid-19th century. Two young men from the district, Michael Coleman (1891-1945) and James Morrison (1893-1947), absorbed the music around them and added their own individual refinements to what they heard.

Both had become fiddle players of outstanding ability by the time they emigrated to the United States where their music was committed to 78-rpm records from the early 1920s.

Even as a boy, Coleman's fiddle-playing talent was noted locally as special. Some people explained his genius as a gift that had been bestowed on Michael and his older brother, Jim, by the fairies. Their encounter with the Otherworld was said to have taken place when the brothers were returning home late at night after a music session in a neighbour's house in Killavil. A local resident P.J. Duffy took Harry Bradshaw to the fields where the young Coleman had been 'touched' with the gift of music that night. The use of the expression 'touched' is not uncommon to this day in Ireland and is widely understood to infer some form of otherworldly intervention more often than not attributable to the fairies.

P.J. Duffy was born in Killavil, Ballymote, County Sligo, and is a renowned local historian. He has written on the history of the local area and is an authority on Sligo music and musicians. For many years, he has been involved with the Coleman Music Centre in Gurteen, County Sligo as a collector of music and folklore.

Harry Bradshaw is a former radio producer with RTÉ the Irish public service broadcasting organisation, which he joined in 1968. He is a sound engineer and specialises in remastering sound recordings, particularly in the area of traditional music. Harry was recipient of Gradam na gCeoltóirí (Musicians' Award) of TG4, the Irish-language television station in 2008. He has produced numerous radio programmes related to Irish music and oral tradition and has undertaken a substantial amount of fieldwork. He has also established his own company, Viva Voce, which publishes remastered recordings.

The Otherworld *Music & Song from Irish Tradition*

The Otherworld *Music & Song from Irish Tradition*

Michael Coleman

When I was young they'd send for a little man when they'd be about to build a house. His name was Mickey Neill and they used to say he was going with them. They'd send for him and he'd know if there was a pass where they were going to build – a pass for the dead or for the good people.

Then they'd put down the pegs and leave them for so many nights. If they weren't removed by the end of that time they'd know that they could build away.

Told by Alice Ryan (73), Toome, Limerick to Peadar Ó Domhnaill, 24.10.1937. (NFC 407: 266)

The 'them' that Alice Ryan refers to in her short piece above are the 'good people' or the fairies. To this day in Ireland many people can be reticent to specifically name the fairies. In parts of Ireland, for example, we know that mothers calling their children in from play would not name them directly for fear that the fairies would have power over the children or might attempt to abduct them. Alice Ryan here mentions a specific man who was believed to consort with 'the good people' and possessed knowledge of passes, pathways or roads used by the fairies - more often than not invisible to the human eye. To risk upsetting the otherworldly creatures particularly when starting a major undertaking like building a house was considered most unwise.

P.J. Duffy

The Boys of the Lough and The Merry Blacksmith

played on the fiddle by Michael Coleman

This is one of Michael Coleman's earliest and most popular medleys and is from the publication *Michael Coleman 1891-1945*. Through his recordings, made during the 1920s and 1930s, Coleman became one of the most influential traditional musicians of the twentieth century. He recorded these two reels on the Vocalion label in April 1922. The first tune in the set is 'The Boys at the Lough', more commonly known as 'The Boys of the Lough'. It can be found in Breandán Breathnach's *Ceol Rince na hÉireann, 1*, and a version with the title 'The Rose of Castletown' was published in the Roche Collection. Captain Francis O'Neill included the second tune in this set - 'The Merry Blacksmith' - in *The Dance Music of Ireland*. Other titles for it include 'Paddy on the Railroad' and 'Devils of Dublin'. Cape Breton fiddle players, Johnny Wilmot and Winston Fitzgerald recorded a version of the tune with the title 'Mist on the Loch'.

———

A blacksmith is the only man that can cure a disease that horses have – it is called 'the Monday morning disease'. It is a swelled leg and it is also called 'the weed'. In curing it he opens the toe vein and lets the blood flow till he comes to the good blood. That is a thing that vets won't do or approve of. It relieves the horse at once and the animal is working perfectly after nine days. But if a vet touches the horse at all it won't work for three months.

Told by Joseph McEntee (46), blacksmith, Crossreagh, Mullagh, County Cavan to P. J. Gaynor, 2.1.1942. (NFC 815:50-51)

A blacksmith in his forge, Clonmel, County Tipperary, 1988.

The Otherworld *Music & Song from Irish Tradition*

Lore collected in Cavan presents us here with the belief that the blacksmith had special powers not given to others. A belief in the ability to 'cure', whether an animal or human, was sometimes invested in the smith, other times in 'wise women'. 'Mná Ultacha', or women from the north, referred to women with supernatural or special healing powers. The notion of the sinister north and the benevolent south was common in folk belief.

Forge water was sometimes thought to have protective properties, the smith's anvil might have curative powers and a smith's curse was to be feared. Persons who brought about cures were rarely paid in money.

The Otherworld Music & Song from Irish Tradition

Wayside cairn, Erris, County Mayo, 1949. Passing travellers often added a stone to an existing mound or cairn at a place associated with death or supernatural encounters.

36

Cruel Willie

sung by Stephen Murphy

There was a rich farmer in this town did dwell,
He had a handsome daughter, there was few could her excel,
She was courted by Willie, a sailor so dear,
And Willie by trade was a head engineer.

The queen wanted seamen and young Willie had to go,
Saying: 'Arise lovely Molly and come along with me,
And before we get married our friends we'll go see.'

They roamed through the mountains and that valley so deep,
When innocent Molly she began for to weep,
Saying: 'Willie, cruel Willie, you have lead me astray,
And it's all for one purpose my life to betray.'

'Oh, Molly, lovely Molly, your opinion 'tis right,
For I have been digging your grave all the night.'
They advanced a little further and there she did spy,
A grave freshly dug and a spade lying by.

'Oh, Willie, cruel Willie, you're the worst of all men,
If this be the cold grave I have to lie in,
May the great God reward you when I'm dead and gone.'

When Willie done this deed, sure he quickly went home,
Leaving no-one to bewail her but the small birds alone,
And 'twas on board a ship he went the next day,
And that ship not being well anchored got wrenched o'er the way.

Now one of the sailors, a young Thomas Steward,
Who accidently happened to be out on the moor,
When a beautiful vision he saw standing there,
And she held in her arms a baby so fair.

He being merry in liquor he ran to embrace,
For he never before saw so beauteous a face,
But the vision of Molly soon vanished away,
And straight to the captain he went the next day.

'Oh, captain, captain, a vision I saw last night,
And it gave all our sailors a terrible fright,
For I fear she must have been murdered by one of the crew,
Or else her fair features, I would them have knew.'

The captain called up his men by one, two and three,
But falsehearted Willie, what harm knew he,
Till the vision of Molly before him did stand,
Saying: 'Don't spare him captain, for he is the man!'

The Otherworld *Music & Song from Irish Tradition*

He fell upon his knees and for mercy did crave,
Saying: 'I will go down with you in that very same grave.'
And he got such a shock and a terrible fright,
This young man fell sick and he died the next night.

Now down in yonder valley, yonder valley so deep,
This fair one was found, causing many for to weep,
And she held in her arms a baby so fair.
Her parents may weep for their own Molly dear.

The Otherworld Music & Song from Irish Tradition

This stone in Donard, County Wicklow is known locally as 'St Kevin's Foot', 1982. Water, which gathered in a hollow in the stone was thought to have curative powers. A local man said the original stone was damaged by a farmer who worked in a nearby quarry. Shortly afterwards, he was involved in an accident in which he lost three toes.

Songs sometimes depict crimes of passion. Murder, revenants and the death of the perpetrator of such crimes can feature. This song is also known as 'The Cruel Ship's Carpenter' and 'The Gosport Tragedy' and is an international ballad. The collector, Tom Munnelly, summarised the song in the following manner:

> Willie, a sailor and chief engineer, courts Molly. He is called to sea, but before he goes, he calls on her at daybreak and tells her to come with him to see some friends before they marry. He has been digging her grave all night. He kills her and goes home. He goes on board ship, which is then wrecked. Her ghost appears with a baby to a sailor who is merry in liquor. He goes to embrace her but she disappears. He tells the captain who guesses she was murdered by one of his crew. He calls the men together and the ghost appears before William. He says he will go to his grave with her, sickens and dies. In yonder valley the bodies of Molly and her baby are found. Her parents may weep for her.

The song illustrates matters of justice and retribution. Some of the motifs also find echoes in other songs that treat of seduction followed by murder and the return of the girl's ghost. One such example is the Irish song 'Maile Ní Maileoin' which tells of Maile's seduction and subsequent murder. In 'Maile Ní Maoileoin' the murdered girl appears to her killer to warn him of his impending arrest. Tom Munnelly collected other versions of 'Cruel Willie' and the following summaries indicate some of the motif variation in different versions. A circus worker, Francis Cox, sang a version of the song called 'In London's Fair City' for Tom Munnelly in Leitrim in 1971 and Tom summarised it as follows:

> Sailor courts Molly Brown. He calls on her at daybreak and tells her to come with him to see some friends before they marry. He draws a penknife from his pocket and rips her in two. He goes on board ship. (Her ghost appears) and the ship cannot sail because there is a murderer on board. Two sailors deny that they are murderers but he confesses. He is already married with a wife and a child. (She takes him away with her). He asks to be buried under yon tree.

The many versions of 'Cruel Willie' collected by Tom Munnelly are testament to the popularity of the song in Ireland where it has a number of titles. A building worker, John Candy, from Carlow, was recorded by Tom in 1974, singing a version entitled 'The Rich Merchant' which is very similar to the song sung by Stephen Murphy, as was also the version with an almost identical title 'There Being a Rich Merchant' recorded from John Murphy, a building worker, in Wicklow in 1975. That same year, Tom recorded 'There Was a Rich Merchant' from Johanna Stokes, aged eighty-five, a settled Traveller who was living in Longford. Another Traveller, Larry Mohan, sang a version entitled 'In Dublin's Fair City' in Clones, County Monaghan in 1972, as did Bridget MacDonagh, also a Traveller, in Louth in 1973.

Stephen Murphy was born on the 13th May 1913 and lived and worked in Rathvilly, County Carlow all his life. He and his wife Maura had seven children, three girls and four boys. A lover of nature, he also fished, played music and sang. He worked until two days before his death, on 10 June 1985. Tom Munnelly recorded this song from Stephen in his garage in Rathvilly on the 26th June, 1973 and wrote in his diary entry for that day:

Stephen Murphy

Met Paddy O'Donoghue in Rathvilly. The first man he brought me to was Andy Sibald in the town itself. Very old man - took a good while to get some songs from him but pretty good stuff he had.

Also in the town we went to the garage of Stephen Murphy. Stephen at first denied he knew any songs at all. But thanks to Paddy's powers of persuasion, Stephen eventually assented. I was willing to wait until the night to record but Stephen downed tools and left the car he was working in and began to sing. Very good stuff.

When Tom Munnelly recorded this and a further five songs from him, Stephen was around sixty. Stephen learned 'Cruel Willie' from his mother.

The appearance of the ghost of the betrayed lover Molly results in Cruel Willie's shameful admission of guilt for his crime and his death. Justice eventually served through magical or otherworldly intervention is what links the story of 'Cruel Willie' as sung by Stephen Murphy and the curious tale below which can be dated to a time before the great famine of the 1840s.

━━━━━━━

Bhí seanfhear bocht fadó ann agus casadh fear eile dhó agus d'fhiafraigh an fear seo den tseanfhear an raibh aon airgead aige. Agus dúirt an seanfhear nach raibh aon airgead aige. 'Beidh a fhios agamsa,' a deir sé 'an bhfuil nó nach bhfuil.' Rug sé ar an seanfhear agus bhí sé dhá mharú. Agus tháinig neach beannaithe os a chionn. 'Más feall, fillfear,' a deir an t-aingeal, os a chionn. 'Cé air?' a dúirt an fear a bhí ag marú an tseanfhir. 'Ar mhac do mhic i do dhiaidh.' 'Má théann sé chomh fada sin,' a deir sé 'déanfaidh sé ar m'aghaidh.' Mharaigh sé an seanfhear. Agus bhí tom fiodóg ann agus bhí sé a ghabháil á chur faoi sin agus d'éirigh lacha fhiáin agus thosaigh sí ag bualadh a sciathán agus labhair an neach beannaithe os a chionn aríst. 'A fhianaise seo ort, a Dhia agus a lacha.' Bliain ina dhiaidh sin bhí scoláirí a dhul chun na scoile agus d'éirigh an lacha fhiáin agus bhí sí a bualadh a sciathán.

Rith cuid de na páistí chuig an nead ag an tom agus fuaireadar nead mór uibheachaí ann. Bhí sé scríofa ar na huibheachaí ainm agus sloinne an tseanfhir a maraíodh agus ainm agus sloinne an fhir a mharaigh é. Thugadar na huibheachaí chuig an máistir scoile agus dúradar leis go bhfuaireadar nead lachan agus go raibh ainm agus sloinne a leithéide seo de sheanfhear ar na huibheachaí agus ainm agus sloinne an fhir a mharaigh é. Dúirt an máistir scoile leo a thíocht leis agus an nead a thaispeáint dó. Fuadar leis agus thaispeánadar dó í. Thóig sé leis ina hata na huibheachaí agus thug sé chuig na gardaí iad. Agus chuadar sin go dtí an fear agus é go socair suaimhneach ina theach, gan cuimhne ar bith aige ar an rud a rinne sé. Thug na gardaí leo iad agus leagadh os comhair na cúirte iad. Agus ba iad na huibheachaí a chroch é.

Mairéad Seoighe (60), An Tamhnach Mhór, Leitheanach, Srath Salach, Contae na Gaillimhe a d'inis do Bhrian Mac Lochlainn 1.12.1936. Chuala Mairéad an scéal seo óna máthair i Leitheanach in 1896 nuair a bhí a máthair trí scór bliain d'aois. (CBÉ 271: 167-169)

A poor man long ago met another man and asked him if he had any money. And the old man said he had no money. 'I'll find out if you have or have not,' he said. He caught hold of the old man and set about killing him. And a holy creature came over them. 'An evil deed will rebound,' said the angel above him. 'On whom?' said the man who was killing the old man. 'Down through the generations.' 'So be it,' he said, 'so be it.' He killed the man. And there was a clump of reeds there and he was going to bury him there and a wild duck rose and began flapping its wings and the holy creature spoke above him again asking that both God and the duck bear witness to the crime. A year after that, a group of school children were going to school and the wild duck rose again and flapped its wings. Some of the children ran to the nest under the bush and found a large number of eggs. Written on the eggs were the name and surname of the man who was murdered and the name and surname of the man who murdered him. They brought the eggs to the schoolmaster and told him they had found a duck's nest and that this particular man's name and surname were written on the eggs and the name and surname of his murderer. The schoolmaster told them to come along with him and to show him the nest. They went with him and showed it to him. He took the eggs in his hat and brought them to the police. And they went to the man who was quite comfortable in his house with no thought of what he had done. The police took them and they were brought in evidence to the court. And he hanged because of the eggs.

Told by Mairéad Seoighe (60), An Tamhnach Mhór, Leitheanach, Srath Salach, County Galway to Brian Mac Lochlainn, 1.12.1936. Mairéad heard the story from her mother in Leitheanach in 1896 when her mother was sixty years old. (NFC 271: 167-169)

The magical appearance of eggs in the nest of the duck who has witnessed the murder of the old man leads to the capture and hanging of the wrongdoer. Eggs, perhaps in part because they are sometimes symbols of fertility, were thought to have special powers and were used in divination practices and in cures. In this particular instance, the discovery of the eggs leads to the detection of the murderer.

˙coat Loose

˙old by Seán Ó Catháin

The Otherworld *Music & Song from Irish Tradition*

Ó Choilleagán ba ea Petticoat Loose... agus chuir sí páistí chun báis agus gach aon rud mar sin, ach níor dhamnaigh aon cheann acu san í. Is é an rud a deir siad linn a dhamnaigh í - fuair sí bás maidin Domhnach agus Aifreann á rá in Coilleagán agus í ar meisce agus í chun páiste a bheith aici. Sin é a dhamnaigh í. Insa deireadh bhí na sagairt as a diaidh agus cuireadh amach insa bhFarraige Dearg seacht bliana í agus nuair a bhí na seacht bliana suas tháinig sí isteach arís.

Dúirt Seán Ó Catháin nárbh fhios ceart cé acu Catháin nó hIcí a hainm agus nach raibh aon rud a dhein aon bhean riamh sa saol nár dhein sí. De réir an tseanchais aige bháigh sí máistir scoile Choilleagáin agus chuir sí páistí chun báis. Ba í an eachtra i gCoilleagán maidin Domhnaigh a dhamnaigh í. Bhí sí ag imeacht thimpeall na háite seo chun gach aon áit agus 'dá chasfaí leat san oíche í chuirfeadh sí chun báis tú mura beadh aon rud beannaithe ort. Bhí sí in Caol na Seasc, bhí sí aige Béal Each agus thimpeall Modheilge. Casadh le

go leor daoine í.' Nuair a tháinig sí isteach aríst ní bhfaigheadh sí dul isteach go dtí aon tigh a bheadh coileach istigh roimpi.' Aon tigh bheadh coileach ann ní bhfaigheadh sí dul isteach ar aon chor ann. Ach chuaigh sí isteach go dtí an tigh seo thimpeall Seanlphobal agus lean an sagart í agus nuair a cheist sé í cad a dhamnaigh í dúirt sí leis: "Tá mé tar éis é a rá." Dúirt sé léi go gcuirfeadh sé amach go deo í go dtí an lá tar éis lá an bhreithiúntais aige béal na Farraige Dearga. Dúirt sí sin leis go dh'iompódh sí aon árthach a raghadh ann agus dúirt an sagart léi go gcuirfeadh sé é sin insa tslí ná dh'iompódh sí aon árthach go gcuirfeadh sé cruach iarainn anuas uirthi agus thabharfadh sé obair i d'fhéachaint(?) di, chuirfeadh sé ag déanamh súgán den ghaineamh í go dtí an lá tar éis lá an bhreithiúntais.'

Tá cuid mhór finscéalta sa bhéaloideas faoi 'Petticoat Loose' mórán tagairtí don phearsa seo i gCnuasach Bhéaloideas Éireann. Samhlaítear cuid de na finscéalta agus de na móitífeanna a bhaineann le Petticoat Loose agus le spioraid

Caoimhín Ó Danachair in the archive of the Irish Folklore Commission, 1940s.

bhaineanna eile i gCúige Mumhan. Tagann cuid mhór de na finscéalta agus de na móitífeanna seo chun solais sa traidisiún béil idirnáisiúnta agus iad nasctha leis an Diabhal. Creidtear gur bhean mhímhorálta ba ea Petticoat Loose a chuir coireanna i gcrích agus gur ghearr sagart pionós uirthi astu. Creidtear i gcónaí go mbíonn a spiorad le braith in áiteacha áirithe. Tá mionstaidéar déanta ar Petticoat Loose maille le hanailís ar a ról i reiligiún agus i gcreidiúint an phobail in Éirinn chomh maith leis an bpeirspictíocht fhorleathan Eorpach. (Féach O'Connor, 2005).

Feirmeoir ab ea Seán Ó Catháin a bhí ina chónaí sa Chnoc Buí, Port Láirge. I measc an ábhair eile a thóg Caoimhín Ó Danachair uaidh ar cheirnín aiceatáite i Meitheamh 1948 bhí stair áitiúil, cuntas faoi Na Connerys, faoi mhná sa cheantar a raibh cáil orthu – ina measc Máire Dháltúin agus Máire Ní Annagáin – maille le seanchas logánta eile. Fuair Seán Ó Catháin bás Lá Fhéile Pádraig 1963 agus é in aois sé bliana déag agus trí scór. Is ar éigean atá aon rian den tigh le feiscint inniu. Sna nótaí faoi na daoine ar bhailigh sé ábhar uathu, luann Pádraig Ó Milléadha in 'Seanchas Sliabh gCua' gur tobar béaloideasa é an Cnoc Buí áit a bhfuil cónaí ar Sheán Ó Catháin ar 'bhruach an tobair'. Scríobh sé go raibh 'togha an eolais' ag Seán ar an aimsir a bhí imithe.

Petticoat Loose

Petticoat Loose was from Coilleagán. She killed infants and such like, but none of those things caused her damnation. We are told the cause of her damnation was that she died one Sunday morning while Mass was being said in Coilleagán when she was drunk and about to have a child. That's what damned her. In the end, the priests were after her and she was sent to the Red Sea for seven years and when the seven years were up she returned.

Seán Ó Catháin said that it was not certain if Petticoat Loose's surname was Catháin or hIcí but said she did everything imagineable. Seán related that, among other crimes, she drowned a school master in Coilleagán and killed infants. Her action one Sunday morning during Mass in Coilleagán was what damned her. She was going around everywhere in the district and if you met her at night she would kill you if you weren't wearing something blessed. She was in Caol na Seasc, she was in Béal Each and around Modheilge. Many people encountered her. On her return from the Red Sea she could not enter a house where there was a cock. Any house where there was a cock present, she was not able to enter at all. But she went into this house in Seanphobal and the priest followed her and when he questioned her as to what had caused her damnation she said to him: 'I have said it.' He told her he would banish her to the mouth of the Red Sea until the day following judgement day . She told him that she would overturn any vessel that would pass that way and the priest told her that she would not overturn any vessel, that he would put an iron crook over her and he would give her the job of making ropes of sand until the day after the day of judgement.

A number of legends surround Petticoat Loose. The National Folklore Collection contains numerous references to this female character and some Petticoat Loose legends and motifs are associated with other female spirits also from Munster. Many of these legends and motifs are found in international oral tradition where they are connected with the Devil. It is believed that Petticoat Loose was a 'fallen' woman who committed crimes for which she was punished by a priest. Her spirit is still believed to haunt certain places. A detailed study of Petticoat Loose including an analysis of her role in Irish folk religion and belief in addition to the broader European perspective has been published. (See O'Connor, 2005).

Seán Ó Catháin was a farmer and lived in An Cnoc Buí, County Waterford. Oral accounts recorded by Caoimhín Ó Danachair from him on acetate discs in June 1948 included local history, information about the exiled Connerys who are immortalised in song, and accounts of famous local women including Máire Dháltúin and Máire Ní Annagáin, in addition to other lore. Seán Ó Catháin died on St Patrick's Day, 1963 aged seventy-six. Hardly a trace of his house is to be seen today. In the biographical notes on people from whom he collected material the folklore collector, Pádraig Ó Milléadha, mentions in 'Seanchas Sliabh gCua' that An Cnoc Buí is a place rich in folklore. He wrote that Seán was extremely knowledgeable about history.

The Otherworld Music & Song from Irish Tradition

The Otherworld *Music & Song from Irish Tradition*

Loftus Hall, Hook Head, County Wexford, 1997. There is a story told of a mysterious stranger who arrived to play cards here. Late in the night, a glimpse of his cloven hoof betrayed his true identity – the Devil. Similar stories about the Devil are widespread.

Petticoat Loose

played on the fiddle by Darren MagAoidh

A popular song or tune entitled 'Petticoat Loose' existed in England before the mid-eighteenth century and the earliest known reference to the tune in Ireland dates from 1759. It is not known however, if the English tune with this title or tunes of the same title in Irish tradition are directly related to the particular female character of that name in Irish narrative (See O'Connor 2005, 173-175). There are a number of jigs in the Irish music tradition with the title 'Petticoat Loose' and this particular one was published by Captain Francis O'Neill in *The Dance Music of Ireland*. In East Clare the tune is known as 'The Rooms at Dooagh', thought to refer to local caves. A jig with the title 'Petticoat Loose' can be found in Pat Mitchell's collection *The Dance Music of Willie Clancy*. However, it bears no resemblance to the jig played here and is a version of a tune more commonly known as 'Strop the Razor'. O'Neill's *Waifs and Strays of Gaelic Melody* has yet another jig with the title 'Petticoat Loose'. O'Neill credits the origin of the tune to the manuscripts of James O'Neill and in a note to the tune writes that 'Petticoat Loose is an old name for a dance tune'.

Darren MagAoidh is from Mayobridge, near Newry, in County Down. Darren obtained a degree in Music Education from Trinity College in 2010 having studied at Trinity and at the Dublin Institute for Technology. While a student at the Institute, he played traditional music and was organ scholar in Trinity College. Over the years, he studied the fiddle with players such as Jimmy Burns, Jim McKillop and Brendan Gaughran in addition to attending workshops with Brendan McGlinchey.

───────────

Deirtear go mbíodh Petticoat Loose á taispeáint féin in Béal Locha agus go mbíodh sí a déanamh an domhan damáiste dos na daoine do bhíodh ag imeacht an bóthar. Do chuaigh an sagart amach an lá seo agus do chuir sé fios uirthi agus do tháinig sí agus do dh'fhiafraigh sé dhi cad a dhamnaigh í agus dúirt sí gur mharaigh sí leanbh gan baiste. Do chuir sé an díbirt ansan uirthi amach go dtí an bhFarraige Dhearg go dtí lá an Luain agus deirtear gur minic a chuireann sí a ceann aníos agus deireann sí 'an fada uaim lá an Luain?' Deireann na máirnéalaigh go bhfuil éarthacht éigin ag baint leis an bhfarraige sin.

Peaid Corún (63), Crochta, Baile Phíocáin, Déise, Contae Phort Láirge a d'inis do Nioclás Breathnach, 22.4.1937. Chuala sé an scéal óna athair in 1897 nuair a bhí a athair sé bliana agus trí scór. (CBÉ 332:169)

It was said that Petticoat Loose was to be seen in Baylough and used to do a great deal of damage to people who travelled that road. The priest went there one day and she appeared and he asked her what had damned her and she said she had killed an unbaptised child. He banished her then to the Red Sea until the day of judgement and it is said that she often puts her head up and says 'How long until the day of judgement?' Sailors say that there is something repulsive about that sea.

Told by Peaid Corún (63), Crochta, Baile Phíocáin, Déise, County Waterford to Nioclás Breathnach, 22.4.1937. Peaid heard the story from his father in 1897 when his father was sixty-six years of age. (NFC 332:169)

In keeping with the body of Petticoat Loose tradition in Ireland, the account above is associated with counties Waterford and Tipperary. It re-enforces the belief that Petticoat Loose was a sinful woman who was damned for the murder of an unbaptised child. The concept of the 'never-ending' as one of the severest forms of punishment is vividly conveyed.

Amhrán na Siógaí [The Song of the Fairies]

sung by Róisín Elsafty

D'éirigh mé amach ar maidin sa drúcht,
Mo chóir is mo chúpla, is mo ghunna i mo láimh.
Thit ceo ar an talamh agus chaill mé mo chúrsa,
Agus chuaigh mise amú idir cnoc agus gleann.

Cé chífinn gabháil tharm ach Maile chiúin álainn,
Ba deise í is ba bhreáichte, is bhí a folt mar an ór,
Gur labhair sí go meangach dhom is thug sí
cuireadh go fáiltiúil,
Is thug sí dhom fáirnis i mbia agus chun ceoil.

Bhí a bord ar a hallaí, bhí chuile shórt bia ann,
Is bhí ancaird mór fíona ann a líonfadh naoi
gcáirt, Agus dar brí mo charabhata air
nuair a chaith mé mo dhícheall leo,
Is é an ród úd na miasa é a bhí ag imeacht den chlár.

Chóirigh sí an leaba le bratachaí síoda,
Agus dúirt sí liom síneadh agus codladh go sámh,
Ach nuair a fuair mise amach ó, go raibh mé sa mbruíon,
Is gurb shiúd í an bhean sí bhí ag Fionnbhearra amháin.

'Éirigh i do shuí, a mhic chailligh ó,
Agus gluaisfeadsa aníos as doras do 'hall',
Tá Fionnbhearra geanúil ag tíocht lena shluaití,
Is níor mhaith liom a bhualadh faoi riachtan mo cháis.'

Cé chasfaí i dteach mé ach tigh Pheadair Uí Ómach,
Bhí cearca go leor ann, gan coileach gan ál,
Thosaigh mé ag piocadh thar thimpeall an stóil ann,
Is tháinig an leon ann is dúirt sé; 'a ghrá'.

Nó an cíoradóir, racadóir, meannadóir, mánlóir,
Nach b'ann a bhí ól agus déanamh go grinn.
Bhí long faoina cholainn ann, is bhí bord faoina seolta ann,
Bhí an broc agus an rón ann agus cathaoir na mná.

Má théann tú thar hallaí, téigh hallaí na cúirte,
Bí as is bí ag siúl go n-éirí an lá,
Go Caisleán an Bharraigh má théann tú don seol sin,
Beidh tú as cumhacht a bhfuil i gCnoc Meá.

Déantar cur síos san amhrán ar ar tharla nuair a thug bean ón slua sí fear isteach go bruíon an lucht sí áit a raibh féasta ar siúl. Scanraigh sé nuair a thuig sé gurbh í bean Fhionnbhearra a bhí inti. Is í an chomhairle a chuir sé ar dhaoine coinneáil orthu agus gan a dhul ar strae le fanacht as cumhacht a bhfuil i gCnoc Meá. De réir an tseanchais, is i gCnoc Meá a mhaireann Fionnbhearra agus a shlua sí.

Ó Chonamara ó dhúchas í Róisín Elsafty agus chaith sí blianta i mBaile Átha Cliath. Thug sí tréimhse i mbun an chlub amhránaíochta 'An Béal Binn' i mBré. Tá aithne go forleathan uirthi agus ghnóthaigh sí go leor duaiseanna i réimse an tseann-nóis. Mí Eanáir 2007 a foilsíodh an chéad albam aonair aici 'Má Bhíonn Tú Liom Bí Liom'. Óna máthair, Treasa Ní Cheannabháin, a thug sí cuid mhór de na hamhráin agus den amhránaíocht léi. Is iad na hamhráin ghrá is ansa léi.

Chuala Róisín an t-amhrán seo ó thaifeadadh de Mháirtín Ó Tuathail a rugadh in 1871 sa gCoill Rua, paróiste an Chnoic, Contae na Gaillimhe. Ba é Leo Corduff an rinne an taifeadadh ar an 12ú Meitheamh, 1958 do Choimisiún Béaloideasa Éireann nuair a bhí Máirtín ina chónaí in 5 Lána na Céibhe, Gaillimh. Bhí roinnt línte eile sa leagan den amhrán a bhí ag Máirtín Ó Tuathail agus tharlódh go raibh ceathrúnaí eile arís ag an té a thug an t-amhrán do Mháirtín.

The Song of the Fairies

The song tells how a man loses his way in the mist and fog and is enticed by a fairy woman to the fort of Fionnbhearra, king of the fairies. A feast is taking place in the fort and the man is invited to attend. The mortal man becomes afraid as he realises he has entered the Otherworld and that the fairy woman is Fionnbhearra's wife. He advises people not to go astray and to avoid coming under the power of those who live in Cnoc Meá, a mountain near Athenry, County Galway where Fionnbhearra and his host are reputed to live.

Róisín Elsafty is from Conamara and spent a number of years in Dublin. For some time she was director of the traditional singers' club 'An Béal Binn' in Bray, County Wicklow. She is a well-known singer and has been awarded numerous prizes for sean-nós singing. Her first album was released in January 2007 entitled *Má Bhíonn Tú Liom Bí Liom*. She learned many of her songs from her mother, Treasa Ní Cheannabháin. Róisín prefers the lyrical love songs to other song types. Róisín heard 'Amhrán na Siógaí' on a recording of Máirtín Ó Tuathail who was born in 1871 in An Choill Rua, in the parish of An Cnoc in Cois Fharraige, County Galway. The recording was made by Leo Corduff for the Irish Folklore Commission on the 12th of June, 1958 when Máirtín was living at 5 Quay Lane, Galway. Máirtín Ó Tuathail included some additional lines in his version of the song, but the lines are unclear.

Ríonach uí
Ógáin

Róisín Elsafty

I set out one morning in the dew,
With my gear, my brace and my
gun in my hand,
The mist came and I lost my way,
And I went astray between hill and valley.

Whom did I see passing but quiet,
beautiful Maile,
She was the nicest, the most beautiful,
with hair like gold,
She spoke guilefully and then invited
me in a welcoming fashion,
And she gave me an account of a feast.

There was a table in the hall with all
kinds of food,
There was a large tankard of wine that would
fill nine quarts,
And indeed when I did my best endeavour,
The dishes were cleared from the table.

She made the bed with silk sheets,
And she told me to lie down
and sleep peacefully,
But then I discovered I was in
the fairy dwelling,
And that she was the fairy wife
who was Fionnbhearra's alone.

'Arise, son of the old woman,
And I will go from the door of the hall,
Loving Fionnbhearra is coming with his host,
And I would not like to burden him with my
situation.'
Whose house should I go into but
the house of Peadar Ó hÓmach,
There were lots of hens there,

without a cockerel or a flock,
I began mooching around the stool there,
And the hero came there and said:
'My darling'.

Are you a comber, a raker, a cobbler,
or a tiller,
There was drinking and merrymaking,
There was a ship with its hull and a deck
under the sails,
The badger was there and the seal
and the chair of the woman.

If your are passing, pass by the halls
of the court,
Keep on and stay walking until daybreak,
If you go to Castlebar if that is the
route you take,
You will be beyond the power of
every being in Cnoc Meá.

———————

*Bhí lanúin anseo fadó ó shin agus nuair a bhí
siad bliain pósta bhí siad ag feitheamh ar dhuine
clainne. Tháing an t-am agus mar shíl siad féin,
fuair an bhean agus an páiste bás, ach ní bás a
fuair siad. Badh é an rud a tugadh as iad. Bhí
deirfiúr don bhean seo amuigh fán chnoc ag baint
beairtín luachra ag bun creige agus níor mhothaigh
sí ariamh gur thúsaigh an ceol ins an bhinn os
a cionn. D'éist sí ar feadh tamaill agus chuala sí
bean na binne ag cealgadh an linbh istigh. Shíl an
deirfiúr go dtuigfeadh an bhean amuigh an scéal i
gan fhios don bhunadh a thug as í, ach níor thuig.
Seo é an t-amhrán a bhí aici ag cealgadh an linbh:*

Cnoc Meá,
County Galway,
2012, where
Fionnbhearra,
king of the fairies
is said to live.

The Otherworld *Music & Song from Irish Tradition*

Bliain is an oíche aréir a tugadh
ó m'fhear mé,
Ár ngnúis le chéile ó shin ní fhaca muid,

Huis-a bá-lí agus huis-a-bá -í,
Huis-a bá -í agus codail a leanbh bán.

Tá min eorna agam, is tá min choirce
agam,
Is tá min seagail le dortadh amach agam.

A dheirfiúr dhílis, is a dheirfiúr
charthanach,
Siúd chugat an fear mór is a scian faoina
ascaill leis.

Níor sníomhadh an gréasán caol ná
garbh,
Ach dhá shlait déag a chuaigh ar stéis mo
leanbh bán.

A dheirfiúr dhílis is a dheirfiúr
charthanach,
Ceangal an beartín agus bí ag gabháil
abhaile leis.

A dheirfiúr dhílis is a dheirfiúr
charthanach,
Ní rachaidh mé a choíche go Baile
Uí Iodharláin.

A dheirfiúr dhílis is a dheirfiúr
charthanach,
Bris an t-iarann agus caith a barr orm.

Níor ith mé greim agus níor ól mé
deoch acu,
Ach na preátaí fuarbhruite a bhí ar
dhriosiúr m'athara.

Tá mo leaba cóirithe is an luachair craite
agam,
Is Iníon Uí Mhórtha le theacht ar cuairt
chugam.

*Máire Ní Cheallaigh, An Baile Mór, Teileann,
Contae Dhún na nGall a thug do Sheán
Ó hEochaidh i lár na gcaogaidí.
(CBÉ 1412:94-95)*

There was a couple here long ago and when
they were a year married they were expecting
a child. At the birth, the woman and the child
died, or so they thought.

But they were not dead. They had been taken
away. A sister of this woman was gathering
rushes on the hillside at the foot of a rock and
she heard nothing until the music began in the
hill above her. She listened for a while and she
heard the woman on the hill singing a lullaby
to the child inside. The sister thought the
woman outside would understand the situation
unbeknown to those who had taken her away
but she did not. This is the song she was singing
to the child:

A year from last night I was taken away
from my husband,
Since then we have not seen each
other's faces.

Huis-a bá-lí and huis-a-bá -í,
Huis-a bá -í and sleep my fair child.

I have barley meal and oatmeal,
I have rye meal to pour out.

My dear, kind sister
Here comes the big man towards you
with his knife under his arm.

Neither a fine nor rough web
has been woven,
But twelve feet for my fair child.

My dear, kind sister
Tie up the little bundle and
bring it along home with you.

My dear, kind sister
I will never again go to Baile Uí Iodharláin.

My dear, kind sister,
Break the iron and throw its point at me.

I haven't drunk a drop nor taken a bite
with them,
Only the cold, cooked potatoes
on my father's dresser.

My bed is made and the rushes shaken
down by me,
And Ó Mórtha's daughter is due to
visit me.

*Given by Máire Ní Cheallaigh, An Baile Mór,
Teileann, County Donegal to Seán Ó hEochaidh
in the mid 1950s. (NFC 1412:94-95)*

In Irish tradition, song is sometimes a means of conveying coded messages. In the case of this particular song the fairies have stolen a mortal woman. The woman composes and sings the pseudo-lullaby in the hopes of rescue. She says she has not tasted fairy food or drink implying that were she to do so her chances of return to the mortal world would be greatly reduced. This attests to the belief that to stay for a year and a day, or longer, within a fairy fort condemns the mortal to living with the fairies. The abducted woman's plea for the point of the iron to be thrown at her directly references the belief in the power of metal against otherworldly evil.

Boy in petticoat, Inis Meáin, County Galway, 1930. It is thought that young boys were sometimes dressed in skirts to protect them from fairy abduction. A belief existed that the fairies would choose boys before girls.

The Otherworld *Music & Song from Irish Tradition*

The Moving Clouds

played on the fiddle by Néillidh Boyle

Néillidh Boyle (Néillidh Pháidí Néillidh) (1889-1961) was born in Pennsylvania in the United States of America but came home to Donegal from where his people had emigrated. He acquired much of his music and songs from his mother, Neansa Nic Suibhne, who was originally from Cruit. Néillidh and the piper Séamus Ennis were good friends. Néillidh stayed at Ennis' house in Dublin in February 1946 when Ennis was making disc recordings for the Irish Folklore Commission as part of his ongoing fieldwork.

Néillidh once told how he was taken in by the fairies and learned to play fairy music at a fairy wedding. He did not name a particular tune or tunes that he learned from the fairies but he gave details of the kind of music he learned

from them and claimed that it was a beneficial, enriching experience. His telling identifies the spirit of the fairy music with his own playing and with Irish traditional music in general. In a recording made in the 1950s, Néillidh gave the following florid account to collectors Peter Kennedy and Seán Ó Baoill:

It's a gift that was given to the Irish people. The fairies used to play for them. Well, I was one night along with the fairies, and I heard two of the greatest fiddlers ever I heard. They were holding a wedding this night. They thought here I was lost, in this house. I was out for the whole night and I never had such a night in my life, at a fairies' wedding. And they put me drunk. And... I came home here in the morning,

Néillidh Boyle

The Otherworld *Music & Song from Irish Tradition*

and all hands were surprised when I came in. And it was such embellishments of the Irish music I never heard. I was introduced to the fairies by a friend, who met me. He named the fiddlers and all and I remember the names well. One of them was Séamus Mhaitiú and the other was Cnapán an Chnoic (The Stout Lad from the Hill), that was the names. They were two of the greatest fiddlers that were alive in this country in their day. And of course, I was introduced to the fiddlers, and I learned a lot from them - never before did I hear such fiddle playing on this world, as I heard them fiddlers play. They played such wonderful embellishments – they said it was the enchanted music of Ireland that was long ago buried, buried since the days of the bards, and the days of the old pipers. But thanks be to God, they gave me the … they bestowed a lot of their knowledge, and …I've practised since a lot of their styles and I have got that secret.

The reel 'The Moving Clouds' was composed by Néillidh Boyle in the summer of 1942. He commented that he played a 'lovely chord' one day as he was at home in Cró na Sealg. Seeing that the chord had great effect, he proceeded to compose the tune at home 'in the room'. The tune was composed in the key of F but as Néillidh tuned his fiddle upwards, his playing is closer to the key of G. Kathleen Boyle, a granddaughter of Néillidh, plays the tune along with her father, Hughie, on a recent cd entitled *An Cailín Rua*. 'The Moving Clouds' is also identified with the fiddle player Seán McGuire.

———

That's right: Jimetty Rynne was a fiddler, and he lived away up on the mountain in Cool-a-grane, that would be Leitrim; the furthest house up in the mountain. And several nights he'd be called for about twelve o'clock at night. If he was in bed he'd have to get up: these people would call for him to bring him away, away to some spree or some dance, and he'd be left back in the morning. Well, he used to say that he was away with the fairies. Because that would be several nights and the wife used to say:

'Where were you last night?'

'Not one haet,' he says, 'do I know'.

The wife would say to him:
'Where were you last night?'

'Sure I don't know where I was; I was brought away to a spree and I don't know where it was, and I was left back in the morning and that's all I know of it. '...

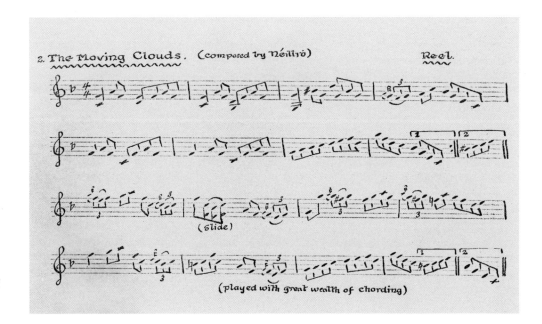

Séamus Ennis' transcription of 'The Moving Clouds', 1944.

*They'd give him some wine: now he could
tell nothing, and he'd play at a spree and
that's all he knew. They'd give him some
of this wine and he'd forget all only just
that he was playing at this spree.*

*Told by Michael Rooney (71), Blacklion,
Kilinagh, County Cavan to Michael J. Murphy
in 1971. (NFC 1786:226-228)*

Although fairy music is often reputed to be
of an exceptionally high standard, the fairies
are sometimes also presented, as requiring the
assistance of a mortal musician. In the preceding
account a mortal living in an isolated, rural area
was called upon at midnight and brought to
play music at a fairy dance. The potency of the
fairy wine caused him to lose track of time in
this otherworld experience.

The Otherworld *Music & Song from Irish Tradition*

'Burning Bush'
(Lone Thorn).
Near Conway's
Forth, Ballintogher,
County Sligo, 1969.

Amhrán an Frag [The Song of the Frog]

sung by Peadar Ó Ceannabháin

Aréir tháinig triúr isteach chugam le titim cheo na hoíche,
Agus d'fhiafraíodar thar éis beannú dhóibh: 'An bhfaca tú an bhean sí?
Mar siúd í a ruaig as baile muid is a ghiorrós lenár saol,
Is ní bheidh beo a bhfuil romhainn go maidin má thagann sí chun an tí.'

Níorbh fhada nó gur chuala muid an siúl isteach sa tsráid,
Is a chomharsanaí na gcarad nach muide a bhí sa ngábh,
Bhí claimhe faoina hascaill is fallaing ar a bráid,
Is ar nós gach uile ghaiscíoch bhí sciath choiseanta ina láimh.

Beidh caint is cáil aríst go brách ar throid na hoíche aréir,
Mar níl aon áit abhus ná thall nach leathfar ann an scéal,
Nár mhór i gceist Cath na bPunann nó an troid a bhí i mBearna an Dúin,
Ach níor thada é do na cearrbhachaí ag iarraidh an taisí a chur ar gcúl.

Chuaigh an troid chun cinn i dtús na hoíche is ceathrar againn a bhí ann,
Ar fud an tí ó thaobh go taobh, anonn agus anall,
Ag iarraidh í a chloí le spreac ná brí ní raibh aon mhaith dhúinn ann,
Ach a bhfuil sa ríocht is bídís cruinn, ní chuirfeadh í ar lár.

Is níl fear ar bith dá bharúlaí dár tóigeadh ariamh san áit,
A bhfaigheadh sí barróg faoi a bharr-easnachaí nach gcuirfeadh sí air breall,
Lena fiacla fada fuara, stróic sí an ghruaig anuas dár gceann,
Níl iarraidh ar bith dá mbuaileadh sí nach dtéadh sí go dtí an chnáimh.

Ach saol fada go bhfágha an Flathartach go brách ná raibh sé tinn,
Mar níl aon uair dá spreagainn é nach neartaíodh sé dhá dtrian,
An uair a bhínnse leagthaí is an taisí os mo chionn,
Gur le neart a lúith is a ghaisce a bhí sé in ann í a chur as greim.

Ach d'imigh sí mar tháinig sí is d'fhág sí muide tinn,
Is an chuid againn nach bhfuil bacach d'fhág sí an arraing ina dhroim,
Ach tá mé cinnte dearfa is cér miste liom é a rá,
Gurb é fear na Maighdine Mara é is é gléasta in éadach mná.

Uaireanta, tagann cúrsaí osnádúrtha i gceist in amhráin ghrinn. Amhrán magúil é seo áit a dtáinig frag isteach i dteach agus ar dearnadh comórtas idir í agus an bhean sí nó pearsa mná ón saol eile a dhéanann an bás a thuar. Tá staidéar ar an mbean sí i dtraidisiún na hÉireann déanta ag Patricia Lysaght (Lysaght 1985).

Ar an 23 Iúil 1942 bhailigh Liam Mac Coisdeala an cuntas seo a leanas ó Mhícheál Bheairtle:

Oíche bhí mé istigh sa teach liom péin san airneán is ní raibh tada den oíche ann nuair a tháinig triúr stócach eile isteach ar cuairt chugam agus bhí muid leagthaí amach ar a dhul ag imirt cluiche cártaí nuair a tháinig frag isteach fud an tí chugainn. Ach d'éirigh an ceathar againn agus chuir muid amach í, mé féin agus fear de Fhlathartach, fear de Chlainn Mac Conaola agus fear de Cheannabhánach. Ach chuir muid amach í ar chuma ar bith agus dhún muid an doras agus tháinig sí isteach aríst agus chuir muid amach í. Ach dúirt mé féin leothub gá dteagadh sí isteach an tríú huair iad a bheith ullmhaithe nach rud ceart ar chor ar bith a bhí ann. Agus ní túisce bhí an focal as mo bhéal ná bhí sí istigh aríst. Agus chaith muid an oíche léi go dtí an dódhéag idir cheithre choirnéalaí an tí agus chinn orainn í a mharú agus d'imigh sí gan bhuíochas dúinn. As sin go ceann cúpla oíche nuair a bhí mo scíth ligthí agam, rinne mé amhrán dúinn féin agus don fhrag.
(CBÉ 850: 340-341)

Ba é Maidhcil (Mícheál) Bheairtle Ó Donncha, Cora na gCapall, Cill Chiaráin (c. 1902 – 1979), a rinne 'Amhrán an Frag'. Is iomaí píosa a rinne Maidhcil. Ba leathdhuine cúpla a bhí ann. Tús na 1960idí chuaigh sé go Sasana áit a raibh sé ag obair ar láithreacha tógála.

Is as Aill na Brón, Cill Chiaráin i gConamara é Peadar Ó Ceannabháin ó dhúchas. Chaith sé ceithre bliana fichead ag obair mar léachtóir i gColáiste Oideachais San Caitríona ar an gCarraig Dhubh, Contae Bhaile Átha Cliath. Amhránaí é a ghlac páirt i gceolchoirmeacha éagsúla in Éirinn agus thar lear agus rinneadh taifeadtaí dá chuid fonnadóireachta ar raidió agus ar teilifís. Tá ábhar scríofa aige agus léachtaí tugtha aige ar an amhránaíocht dhúchasach i gConamara. Mhúin sé cúrsaí ar an bhfilíocht bhéil agus tá sé i mbun taighde le tamall ar fhilithe pobail in Iorras Aintheach. Chuir sé eagar ar an leabhar, 'Éamon a

Búrc: Scéalta' (1983), agus eisíodh a chéad albam 'Mo Chuid den tSaol' i 1997.

The Song of the Frog

The Otherworld is sometimes portrayed in amusing songs. 'Amhrán an Frag' is a comical song in which the frog that came into a house is compared to the banshee or female otherworld deathmessenger prominent in Irish oral tradition. A study of the banshee has been undertaken by Patricia Lysaght (Lysaght 1985).

The song was composed by Maidhcil (Mícheál) Bheairtle Ó Donncha, Cora na gCapall, Cill Chiaráin, County Galway (c. 1902 – 1979). Maidhcil composed several songs. In the early 1960s, Maidhcil went to England where he worked on building sites.

Last night, three visitors arrived at nightfall,
And after greeting me they asked:
'Have you seen the banshee?
Because she drove us from our home
and will shorten our lives,
And none of us will survive until morning
if she comes to the house.'

It wasn't long before we heard
movement coming towards us,
'And my friends, weren't we in a
dangerous situation then?'
She had a sword under her arm and
a cloak around her neck,
And like every warrior she held a
shield in her hand for protection.

There will be talk forever of
last night's events,
As the story will be told in
every place imagineable,
The Battle of the Sheaves or the fight
in the gap of the fort are famous,
But that was nothing compared to the
gamblers trying to keep the apparition back.

The fight developed early in the
night and there were four of us,
All around the house,
from side to side back and forth,
Trying to overcome her by
strength or force was futile,
Nothing in the world, however steady,
could overpower it.

The cleverest man alive who grew
up in the place,
If she were to grasp at his ribs that
she wouldn't make him look foolish,
With her long, cold teeth she tore
the hair from our head,
Each blow she struck went straight
to the bone.

But may Ó Flathartaigh be granted
a long life and never be ill,
Because every time I exhorted him his
strength increased two thirds more,
When I was down with the apparition
above me,
His strength, agility and valour forced
her to loosen her grip.

But she left as she had come and she left
us in a sorry state,
And those of us who are not lame,
she left a stabbing pain in our back,
But I am absolutely certain and I don't
mind stating it
That it was the mermaid's husband
dressed in woman's clothing.

On the 23 July 1942, Liam Mac Coisdeala
collected the following account from Mícheál
Bheairtle:

> One night I was alone in the house for night
> visiting and early on three other young lads
> came in to visit me and we were going to
> play a game of cards when a frog came in
> to us and went all over the house. The four
> of us got up and put it outside, myself and a
> lad by the surname Ó Flathartaigh, a Mac
> Conaola and an Ó Ceannabháin. But we
> put it outside at any rate, and we closed the
> door and it came in again and we put it out.
> But I said to them that if it came in a third
> time they should be prepared as it wasn't any
> normal thing at all. No sooner had I uttered
> the words than it was inside again. And we
> spent the night at it until midnight between
> the four corners of the house and we failed
> to kill it and it left again in spite of us. A few
> nights after that when I had rested, I made a
> song for us and for the frog.
> (NFC 850: 340-341)

Peadar Ó Ceannabháin is from Aill na Brón,
Cill Chiaráin. He spent a number of years as a
lecturer in St Catherine's College of Education,
Blackrock, County Dublin. He has performed at
concerts throughout Ireland and abroad. He has
published and lectured widely on the traditional
singing of Conamara and has also lectured widely
on oral poetry. He is currently researching the
traditional poets of Iorras Aintheach, County
Galway. He edited the book *Éamon a Búrc:
Scéalta* (1983) and his first album *Mo Chuid den
tSaol* was published in 1997.

---

*Scata cailíní óga a bhí ar buaile i
gcionn beithíoch agus chonaic siad frag
suntasach ag gabháil tharthu.*

*'Nach uafásach mór an frag é sin!'
a deir duine acu.*

*'Nach mór an bolg atá air!' a deir ceann
eile acu.*

*Ach bhí cailín géimiúil ann, cailín díchéillí,
agus dúirt sí féin: 'Nár bheire tú an
t-ualach sin choidhchin,' a deir sí,
'go mbeidh mise in do láthair!'*

*D'imigh sin ann féin go ceann trí oíche
ina dhiaidh go ndeachaigh sí ag iarraidh
canna uisce ag an tobar. Nuair a thóg
sí an canna uisce is bhreathnaigh sí os
a cionn chonaic sí duine uasal breá ag
marcaíocht ar chapall bán agus labhair
sé léithe:*

*'Fág an t-uisce ansin, a chailín mhaith,' a
deir sé, 'agus teara uait in éineacht liomsa.'*

'Ní ghabhfad,' a deir sí, 'ná chor ar bith.'

*'Mura dteaga tú le réiteach,' a deir sé,
'caithfidh tú a theacht le haimhréiteach.
Ní thabharfaidh mé i bhfad ó bhaile thú,'
a deir sé, 'agus mo lámh agus m'fhocal
duit,' a deir sé, 'go bhfágfaidh mé slán
sábháilte anseo arís thú taobh istigh
d'uair a chloig.'*

*'Cáil tú do mo thabhairt,' a deir sí, 'nó cén
ghraithe atá agat díom?'*

The Otherworld *Music & Song from Irish Tradition*

'An gcuimhníonn tú ar an gcaint a dúirt tú trí lá ó shin,' a dúirt sé, 'agus tú ar buaile, nuair a chonaic tú an frag mór ag gabháil thart, nuair a ghuibhigh tú gan é a breith ualach go mbeifeá féin ina láthair? Sin é an áit atá mise do do thabhairt anocht. Sin í,' a deir sé, 'bean Fhionnbhearra a bhí ag imeacht faoi dhraíocht. Tá sí i dtinneas páiste anocht,' a deir sé, 'agus ní fhéadfaidh sí é a chur ar an saol go mbeidh tusa ina láthair.'

Chuaigh sí ar chúlóg taobh thiar dhe agus chroch sé leis í. Ní mórán achair a chuadar nuair a tháinig sé suas le aill mhór mhillteach. Bhí aithne agus eolas aici ar an aill chomh maith is bhí aici ar a leathláimh.

D'oscail doras i lár na haille. Isteach le fear an chapaill agus an bhean óg i ngreim láimhe aige. Chonaic sí dubhadh na gcnoc agus breacadh na ngleannta de dhaoine ann. Thug an fear leis í siar trasna na cúirte go dtáinig sé ag ceann staighre a bhí ag gabháil síos i siléar. Thug sé síos an staighre i ngreim láimhe í go dtug sé chuig an bparlús ba bhreátha í dá bhfaca sí riamh le amharc a súl. Thug sé isteach i seomra speisialta í agus bhí bean bhreá óg a raibh cúl rua gruaige uirthi sínte sa leaba agus í ag éagaoin. Ar an bpointe boise is a bhfaca sí an bhean óg seo chuir sí a cúram di agus rugadh an páiste. Bhí áthas mór orthu uilig ansin. Agus bhí an-bhuíochas aici seo ar an mbean óg má b'fhíor dhi féin.

Tháinig máistir na Bruíne thart.

'Tá súil againn anois,' a deir sé, 'go dtabharfaidh tú duais eicín don chailín seo as ucht thú a fhuascailt,' a deir sé, 'agus thú thabhairt slán ó do chúrsa.'

'Níorbh é mo dhearmad é,' a deir sí.

Chuir sí a láimh thairsti suas agus thug sí crios síoda amach ón bpiliúr agus shín sí chuici é.

'Seo dhuit anois, a chailín mhaith,' a deir sí, 'beidh d'athair agus do mháthair an-bhródúil as an duais seo. Ach ní inseoidh tusa go brách cé bhfuair tú é agus ní chuirfidh tú ort é go dté tú abhaile.'

Tháinig an marcach thart a thug sa mBruíon í. Fuair sé greim lámh uirthi.

'Téanaim uait,' a deir sé, 'tá do ghraithe déanta anseo agat. Caithfidh mise bheith suas le mo ghealltanas,' a deir sé, 'agus thú fhágáil san áit a dtug mé as thú.'

Shiúil sé leis an bealach céanna a dtáinig siad isteach. Agus ar an bpointe a raibh siad taobh amuigh den doras ní raibh teach ná cúirt le feiceáil ach éadan na haille mar bhí sí i gcónaí. Chuir sé ar a chúl ar an gcapall í.

'Shílfeá,' a deir sé leis an gcailín óg, 'go bhfuair tú féirín deas ón máistreás.'

'Fuaireas,' a deir sí, 'agus tá mé an-bhródúil as.'

'B'fhiú dhuit sin,' a deir sé, 'dá mbeadh a fhios agat céard tá ann.'

Bhíodar ag dul thar chrann daraí a bhí ag fás i leataobh an bhóthair agus sheas sé an capall.

'Gabh anuas anois,' a deir sé, 'mar dhéanfadh cailín maith. Cuir cor den chrios sin,' a deir sé, 'timpeall ar an gcrann daraí. Ná bí mall leis,' a deir sé, 'ach an oiread.'

Ghabh sí anuas agus chuir sí cor den chrios ar an gcrann daraí agus tháinig sí ar ais go dtí an marcach chomh scafánta is d'fhéad sí. Agus ní raibh sí ar ais nuair a d'airigh sí torann an chrainn daraí ag titim taobh thiar di. Scanraigh sí agus bhreathnaigh sí thairti.

'Ná bíodh faitíos ort,' a deir fear an chapaill. 'Ach féadfaidh tú,' a deir sé, 'a bheith buíoch díomsa anocht. Bí buíoch,' a deir sé, 'gur mé tháinig do d'iarraidh. Marach gur mé,' a deir sé, 'bhí do mhála millte agus do mhargadh déanta agus do chairde ar an saol seo caite! Ar an bpointe,' a deir sé, 'agus a ngabhfása abhaile agus chuirfeá an crios sin faoi do lár i láthair d'athar agus do mháthar, dhéanfadh sé dhá leith dhíot mar dhéanfadh scian de mhioscán ime. Ní mhairfeá leath an achair dó agus mhair an

The wart stone,
Rathbride, County
Kildare,1962. Water
in a hollow in the
stone is believed to
cure warts.

The Otherworld *Music & Song from Irish Tradition*

crann daraí. Agus nár bhocht an bás agat
é le do dhíchéille!'

D'fhág sé ar ais ag an tobar í.

'Tá do chomhairleachan anois agat,' a
deir sé. 'Rud ar bith a fheicfeas tú níos
mó,' a deir sé, ' a mbeidh suntas ar bith
air, ag gabháil fút ná thart, cuimhnigh ar
an seanfhocal: an rud nach mbaineann
duit ná bain dó. Agus sábháilfidh sin thú,'
a deir sé.

D'fhága sé slán aici agus d'imigh sé sna
cosa in airde. Is dá bhfeiceadh sí aon frag
aríst go brách ghabhfadh sí míle as an
gcosán faitíos an gcasfaí léithi í.

Vail Ó Donncha (38), Banrach Ard, Cill Chiaráin,
Contae na Gaillimhe a d'inis do Liam Mac
Coisdeala, 1942. (CBÉ 850: 160-164)

A group of young girls were taking care
of cattle and they saw a big strange frog
going by.

'Isn't that a very big frog!'
one of them said.

'Isn't its stomach very big!'
another one said.

But there was a funloving girl there,
a silly girl and she said:

'Don't give birth,' she said 'until I am
present!'

And so it was until three evenings later she
went to fetch a pail of water at the well.
When she had raised the pail of water she
looked up and saw a fine gentleman on a
white horse and he spoke to her:

'Leave the water there, my good girl,'
he said, 'and come along with me.'

'I will not go,' she said, 'and that is for sure.'

'You must come,' he said. I won't bring
you far from home,' he said, 'but I give
you my solemn word, that I will leave you
back safe and sound within the hour.'

'Where are you bringing me,' she said,
'or why do you need me?'

'Do you remember what you said three
days ago' he said, 'when you were
booleying, when you saw the big frog
going by, and you wished him not to
give birth until you were present? That
is where I am bringing you tonight.
That was' he said, 'Fionnbhearra's wife
who was under a spell. She is in labour
tonight,' he said, 'and is unable to give
birth until you are present.'

She got up on the horse behind him and
he carried her off . It wasn't long before he
arrived at a great big cliff. She knew the
cliff as well as she knew her right hand.

A door in the middle of the cliff face
opened. The horseman went in holding
the young girl by the hand. She saw a
vast crowd of people. The man brought
her through the courtyard until they
reached the top of a stairs that went to a
cellar. He brought her down the stairs to
the finest parlour she had ever seen. He
brought her into a special room where
a beautiful young redhaired woman lay
in labour. As soon as she saw the young
woman in pain she began tending to her
and a child was born. Everyone was very
happy then. And the woman was very
grateful to the young girl.

The master of the fairy fort came in.

'I hope, now, ' he said 'that you will reward
this girl in some way for relieving you,' he
said, 'and for delivering you safely.'

'I have not forgotten,' she said.

She stretched up her hand, took a silk belt
from the pillow and gave it to her.

'Here you are, my good girl,' she said,
'your father and mother will be very
proud of this reward. But you are never to
reveal where you got it and you must not
put it on until you go home.'

The rider who had brought her into the
fairy fort appeared. He took her by the
hand.

'Let us go,' he said, 'you have done your
work here. I will have to keep my promise,'
he said, 'and leave you where I found you.'

He went off the same way he had come in. And as soon as they were outside the door, the court was no longer to be seen, only the face of the cliff as it had always been. He placed her behind him on the horse.

'You would think,' he said to the young girl, 'that you got a lovely present from the mistress.'

'You would think that,' she said, 'and I am very proud of it.'

'You should know then,' he said, 'what it is.'

They were passing an oak tree that was growing on the side of the road and he stopped the horse.

'Get down now,' he said, 'like a good girl. Put a piece of that belt,' he said, 'around the oak tree and don't delay.'

She got down and put some of the belt on the oak tree and came back to where the horseman was as quickly as she could. And she had only just returned when she heard the noise of the oaktree falling behind her. She took fright and looked over.

'Don't be afraid,' said the man with the horse, 'but you can be grateful to me tonight. Be grateful,' he said, 'that it was I came for you tonight. Otherwise, you

would have been in a bad state, your life ended. As soon,' he said, 'as you had arrived home and the belt around your waist in front of your father and mother, it would have cut you in two halves just as a knife would cut a piece of butter. You would not have survived half as long as the oaktree did. And wouldn't that be a sorry end because of your foolishness.'

He left her back to the well.

'You have learned your lesson now,' he said. 'Anything you see around you in the future,' he said, 'that is remarkable in any way, remember the saying: leave well enough alone. And that will save you,' he said.

He said goodbye and sped away. And if ever she saw a frog after that she made a long detour around it in case she might meet it.

Told by Vail Ó Donncha (38), Banrach Ard, Cill Chiaráin, County Galway to Liam Mac Coisdeala, 1942. (CBÉ 850: 160-164)

This cautionary legend was collected by Liam Mac Coisdeala from Mícheál's brother Vail in 1942, the same summer he collected the song 'Amhrán an Frag' from Mícheál. It advises caution when making a wish.

———

If you got a burn and shouted 'O! I am burnt' you could not get the cure, but if you said nothing you went to an old man there beyond that had the cure and said 'lick, lick' and he licked the burn with his tongue. To get the cure he had to get a frog and lick him three times up the back.

Told by Patsy Carrigan (62), Gubaveeny, Killinagh, County Cavan to Séamus A. Ó Dubhláinn, 1935-1936. (NFC 212:262)

The short account above underlines the importance of inherited knowledge and of the importance of ritual and its observance in traditional practice. The curative powers of the tongue and of saliva – human and animal – are well established in folk medicine. Frogs, lizards and mankeepers were used for cures and divination.

Rag-tree, Mohill, County Leitrim, 2010. Rags and pieces of cloth are tied to trees, usually, whitethorn, in the hope of a cure or beneficial intercession.

The Otherworld *Music & Song from Irish Tradition*

The Banshee

told by Mag Doyle

The Banshee was heard regular in Ringsend and the people believed in it. There was a lot of families that when the banshee would cry there would be a death in the family.

Belief in the wailing sound of the banshee (*bean sí*) as a portent of death still exists in Irish tradition and is found in rural and urban communities. Her cry is often said to be associated with families of a particular surname, frequently those surnames which include 'Ó' or 'Mac'. Oral accounts often tell of the banshee being heard by people whose relative in a distant country is about to pass away or has just done so. Sometimes people are warned not to meddle with a comb they might come across as it could belong to the banshee and could therefore bring ill-luck to the discoverer. (See Lysaght 1985).

Mag Doyle (Mrs Bill Higgins), 106 Ringsend Park, Dublin provided several accounts of the banshee and associated belief. In addition, she spoke of other omens of death and of ill luck. Between 1979 and 1980 she contributed a number of hours of lore on the history of Ringsend, on local characters, nicknames, cures, food and much else besides. Mag was in her late seventies when the recordings were made.

This recording was made by Bróna Nic Amhlaoibh and Tony Lynch as part of the Urban Folklore Project (UFP) which was undertaken by various collectors under the auspices of the former Department of Irish Folklore, UCD and was directed by Professor Séamas Ó Catháin. The material now forms part of the National Folklore Collection and it

Street Scene, Ringsend, Dublin 1979.

The Otherworld *Music & Song from Irish Tradition*

consists mostly of personal interviews recorded throughout Dublin and its environs, as well as field recordings made at various city locations. The project helped to redress the earlier focus on largely rural folklore and on material collected in Irish.

Bróna Nic Amhlaoibh is originally from County Armagh. A graduate in Irish Folklore she is former editor of the folklore journal *Sinsear*. She was collector with the UFP for its duration and recorded hundreds of hours of material during this time. She is a former News Editor with the Irish language news service in RTÉ.

———

The 'badhbh' follows the MacInerneys and the O'Briens. The 'badhbh' was heard here a few weeks ago and one of the O'Briens died in a few days after. I heard my mother say that she is a big, tall, white woman with long flowing hair. I don't know the colour of the hair. The 'bean sí' some people call her but I always heard her called the 'badhhh' by my father and mother and the people around Toor.

Told by Johnny Power (40), Réidh Meánach, An Tuar, Déise, County Waterford to Nioclás Breathnach. Johnny heard it from his mother in 1916 when his mother was aged fifty. (NFC 259:518)

The above is a vivid description of the physical appearance of the banshee or 'badhbh' as she is known in certain areas. The word 'badhbh' is variously used in Irish to depict the banshee, a war goddess, a bogeywoman or a scald-crow, forms which convey a sense of power, fear and dread.

Mag Doyle

Bróna Nic Amhlaoibh

The Otherworld Music & Song from Irish Tradition

The Banshee Reel

played on the tin whistle by Micho Russell

The Otherworld *Music & Song from Irish Tradition*

Micho Russell (1915-1994) was born in Doonagore, Doolin, County Clare where he lived all his life. His mother played the concertina and his brothers, Gussie and Packie were celebrated musicians in the locality. He related particularly well to people and was very much his 'own man'. He performed at many venues and concerts in Ireland and abroad and was an inspirational teacher. Micho knew Irish and remembered Irish being spoken in the district. The book *Micho's Dozen - Traditional Songs from the Repertoire of Micho Russell, Doolin, County Clare* (collected by Tom Munnelly) was published by the Ennistymon Festival of Traditional Singing in 1991.

The version of 'The Banshee Reel' played here by Micho Russell appears to have been influenced by the music of the Flanagan Brothers, Joe, Mike and Louis, who were one of the leading Irish dance-hall attractions in New York during the 1920s and early 1930s. There is another tune with the title 'The Banshee' also known as 'McMahons Reel'. It can be found in Breandán Breathnach's *Ceol Rince na hÉireann 2*.

Micho Russell

Tá cnoc i gCúil Mhín ar a dtugtar 'Creagán na gCat'. Seo mar a hainmníodh é. Bhí bean sí riamh ag Muintir Uí Loinsigh sa chuid seo den Chlár agus nuair a bhíodh duine acu marbh dheineadh sí a greas caointe i gcónaí ar an gcnoc seo. Dheineadh sí an caoineadh díreach mar bheadh cait ag gol is ag béiceadh. Uime sin tugadh 'Creagán na gCat' ar an gcnoc.

Scríofa ag D. Ó Murchú, O.S., Scoil Chúil Mhín, Inis, Contae An Chláir, 1938. (CBÉS 603: 272-273)

There is a hill in Cúil Mhín called 'Creagán na gCat' [The Stoney Patch]. This is how it got that name.

The Ó Loinsigh family were always associated with the banshee in this part of Clare and when one of them died she always did a keening session on this hill. She keened just like cats wailing and shrieking. That's why the hill was called 'Creagán na gCat'.

Written by D. Ó Murchú, N.T., Cúil Mhín School, Ennis, County Clare, 1938. (NFCS 603: 272-273)

Micho Russell at St. Brigid's Well, Liscannor, County Clare.

The Otherworld Music & Song from Irish Tradition

Seachrán Sí [Set Astray by the Fairies]

sung by Saileog Ní Cheannabháin

Seachrán sí a bhain dom i dtús na hoíche,
Agus dúirt mo mhuintir uilig gur bréag é,
Ach, dar a bhfuil de bhíoblaí as seo scríofa,
Ar fleidh is ar féasta is ea a chaith mé an
oíche úd.
Bhí togha gach bia ann, bhí rogha gach dí
ann,
Bhí bairillí fíona ann dhá roinnt is
dhá réabadh,
Is nár mhór an t-iontas a dhéanfadh
daoine saolta,
Den chulaith shíoda a bhí ar mo Bhéibí.

Is ar mo theacht dhom isteach don pharlús,
Cuireadh fáilte mhór is céad romham,
Is d'iarr sí am beag le theacht i láthair,
Is paca cártaí, dá mb'fhéidir.
'Gabhaim pardún agat, a ógmhnaoi mhánla,
Níl an spás agam go deo le déanamh,
Mar tá mo mháirseáil go Baile Tigh Ardáin,
Ag faire ar mhná breátha mar Bhéibí.'

'Muise, dímhúinte ort, céard a dúirt tú?
Glan do shúile nach mise Béibí?
Agus níl do ghráínsa i mBaile Tigh Ardáin,
Ach seoideog [séideog] fhánach a fágadh
aréir ann.
Ó, suigh síos is caith bia linn,
Is fearr bainis go mór ná tórramh,
Agus cá bhfuil na véarsaí breátha a
ghabh tú aréir di,
A Mhr Grady, is tú ag gabháil na móinte?'

Níor chuir mé suim ina raibh dhá rá liom,
Go bhfaca mé an lánúin dhá gcur le chéile,
I ngreim barr láimhe ag tíocht don pharlús,
Is fillte an gháire ní raibh in mo Bhéibí.

Tá de chumhacht ag na daoine maithe daoine saolta a chur ar strae ar bhealaí éagsúla. Faoi mar a dúirt Sorcha Ní Ghuairim faoin amhrán: 'Bean óg a tugadh as atá i gceist san amhrán seo. Bhí sí ag gabháil a phósadh agus bhí an fear a bhí sí le phósadh ag gabháil ag breathnú uirthi nuair a tugadh isteach sa mbruíon é agus tá an chaint a tharla idir é féin, an bhean, agus na daoine maithe san amhrán. Pósadh os comhair a dhá shúil istigh sa mbruíon í, "leis an bhfear is gránna a shiúil Éirinn"

atá ráite i ndeireadh an amhráin.' Tugtar 'Coillte Uaráin' ar an amhrán freisin.

I measc na gcuntas faoin amhrán, bhailigh Brian Mac Lochlainn an méid seo a leanas do Choimisiún Béaloideasa Éireann sa mbliain 1936, in éineacht le leagan den amhrán, ó Eilís Ní Chonraoi (48), Dúinín, An Clochán, Contae na Gaillimhe:

> *Sin fear a bhí ann fadó agus an oíche a phós, cailleadh a bhean – tugadh as í. Bhí sé ag imeacht ansin go bhfaigheadh sé rudaí le hí a thórramh. Ach thug na daoine maithe isteach sa mbruíon é, ag magadh faoi agus nuair a chuaigh sé isteach, chonaic sé a bhean féin – a bhí caillte. Chuir sí fáilte roimhe agus rinne sí a dícheall ceist a chur air, féachaint an mbeadh sé in ann í a thabhairt as. Sin é an fáth a d'iarr sí cluiche cártaí leis, mar dá ngnóthadh seisean an cluiche, ba leis í – ach níor thuig sé céard a bhí uaithi. Ansin dúirt Conchúr Ó Dálaigh go bpósfadh sé féin í – sin Rí na slua sí agus b'éigin dó ansin imeacht gan í. (CBÉ 271:85)*

Is cainteoir dúchais Gaeilge í Saileog Ní Cheannabháin. Is iad fonnadóirí Iorras Aintheach i gConamara is mó a chuaigh i bhfeidhm ar a cuid fonnadóireachta. Bhain sí céim BMus amach le Coláiste na hOllscoile, Corcaigh, áit ar ghnóthaigh sí Duais Sheáin Uí Riada mar gheall ar thionscnamh ar amhráin agus ar amhránaithe Iorras Aintheach. Casann sí ceol tradisiúnta ar an bhfidil agus ar an bpianó. Tá spéis aici i bhfonnadóireacht as na Gaeltachtaí eile freisin.

Set Astray by the Fairies

I was set astray by the fairies early at night,
And my family said it wasn't true,
But, by all the bibles that have been written,
I spent that night at a banquet and a feast.
There was the best of food, and every kind
of drink,
There were barrels of wine being divided
and being forced open,
Wouldn't mortal beings wonder greatly,
At the silk suit my Béibí was wearing?

When I came into the parlour,
I was welcomed heartily,
And she asked that she might
present herself in short while,
With a pack of cards, if possible.
'I beg your pardon, gracious young woman,
I don't have that much time to give,
Because I have to march to Baile Tigh Ardáin,
Keeping watch over fine women like Béibí.'

'Well, you ignorant person,
what did you say?
Look closely, am I not Béibí?
Your little love is not in Baile Tigh Ardáin,
But it was a stranger was left
there last night.
Sit down and eat with us,
A wedding is far better than a wake.
Where are the fine verses you sang
for her last night,
Mr Grady, as you journeyed
over the marshes?'

I paid no heed to what was being said to me,
Until I saw the couple being joined,
Holding hands together coming into the
parlour,
And my Béibí did not appear laughing.

The fairies have the power to set humans astray in a number of ways. The Conamara singer, Sorcha Ní Ghuairim, sang this song and said it concerns a young woman, who was to be married but was taken away into a fairy rath. The man she was to marry saw her, inside the fairy rath, being married to the ugliest man in Ireland. The song is also called 'Coillte Uaráin'.

The narrative accounts relating to the song include the following, which was collected by Brian Mac Lochlainn for the Irish Folklore Commission in 1936, along with a version of the song, from Eilís Ní Chonraoi (48), Dúinín, Clifden, County Galway:

> There was a man long ago and the night he married, his wife died – she was taken. He was on his way to fetch supplies for her wake. But the good people brought him into the fort for sport, and when he went in, he saw his wife – who had died. She welcomed him and did her utmost to ask him, to see if he could bring her away. That's why she asked him for a game of cards, because if he won the game, she was his – but he didn't understand what she wanted. Then Conchúr Ó Dálaigh said he would marry her himself – he was the King of the fairy host – and he had to leave then without her. *(NFC 271:85)*

Saileog Ní Cheannabháin's greatest influence has been the singers of Iorras Aintheach in Conamara. She gained a BMus degree in University College Cork in 2009 and was also awarded the Seán Ó Riada Prize for her project on the songs and singers of Iorras Aintheach. She plays the fiddle and plays traditional and classical music on the piano. Saileog is also interested in songs and singing from other Irish-speaking districts.

Saileog Ní
Cheannabháin

The Otherworld Music & Song from Irish Tradition

There's a spot in Charlestown in Barrack St. outside Mills' and anybody that stands on it will be led astray. When they meet someone they know they'll regain consciousness.

When put astray you should, according to a traditional prescription, turn your coat inside out that you may find your way. In bogs there is what old people call a 'fóidín meara' which is, according to one of my informants, a glow worm, a bit of bog oak illumined at night by phosphorous. Anybody who stands on this is almost certain to be put astray.

Collected by Séamus Ó Piotáin from Miss E. Davitt (33), Dromeda-Joyce, Killasser, County Mayo, 7.11.1935. (NFC 117: 101-102)

The preceding account from County Mayo provides advice for people who might be set astray by otherworld forces. A place where a person might be set astray can be called 'stray sod', 'fóidín mearbhaill' or 'fóidín meara'. The stray sod is often said to mark the spot where an unbaptised child has been buried.

A lone bush surrounded by megaliths marks a revered place in Kilvine, County Mayo.

The Otherworld Music & Song from Irish Tradition

Willie Leonard

sung by John Stokes

On a fine summer's morning, Willie Leonard he rose,
To his comrade's old bedchamber, sure he quickly did go,
Saying: 'It's comrade, loyalest comrade, you let nobody know,
It is a fine summer's morning and bathing we'll go.'

Oh, we walked along together till we came to a lane,
And the first man we met with was the keeper of game,
Oh, saying: 'Where are you going to, or it's don't ye venture in,
For there is deep and false waters in the old lakes of Coolfin.'

Sure young Willie he being so headstrong he had swum the lake round,
He had swum towards an island but not to dry ground,
Saying: 'It's comrade, loyalest comrade, it is now I'm getting weak.'
And those was, oh, the last words young Willie Leonard did speak.

Oh, 'twas early on that morning Willie's sister she rose.
To her mother's old bedchamber sure she quickly did go,
Saying: 'It's mother, dearest mother, sure I had a sad dream,
That young Willie he was floating upon a watery stream.'

Oh, 'twas early on that morning Willie's mother came there,
With the wringing of her fingers and the tearing of her hair.
'Was there anybody looking or was there anybody by,
That would venture, oh, their life, for oh, my own darling boy?'

Oh, 'twas early on the next morning, oh, Willie's uncle came there,
He had swum the lake at large like a man all in despair,
Oh, saying: 'Where was he drownded or else did he fall in?
For there's deep and false waters all in the old lakes of Coolfin.'

Sure the day of Willie's burying oh, there was a sad sight,
There was four and twenty young men and them all dressed in white.
Saying they carried him on their shoulders and they laid him in his clay,
Saying: 'Goodbye Willie Leonard,' and them all walks away.

The Otherworld *Music & Song from Irish Tradition*

John Stokes, a Traveller and horse dealer was twenty-nine years old when Tom Munnelly made the recording on 26th June, 1973 in Baltinglass, County Wicklow, where John was camped. Toms' diary entry reads:

> On the way to Rathvilly, I saw an old-fashioned caravan by the road. The owner, John Stokes, said he had a few songs…Only a couple of songs but a very fine singer.

John was originally from Callan, County Kilkenny and he told Tom he learned this song from his father.

Dreams are often interpreted as portents of the future. People may first become aware of events through a dream. This song is an international ballad in which a drowning is depicted in a dream. It was published by Tom Munnelly on the cassette *Songs of the Irish Travellers, 1967-1975*, European Ethnic Oral Traditions, Trinity College, Dublin, 1983. It is also known as 'The Lakes of Coolfin'. The song is strongly associated with the Barony of Loughinsholin, in south Derry.(See Huntington/Herrmann 1990,146). Tom Munnelly summarised the song in the following manner:

Willie Leonard rises and tells his comrade he is going bathing. They meet a keeper who warns them that there is deep and false water in the Lakes of Coolfin. Willie swims to an island, but not dry ground. His final words are that he is getting weak. Next morning, Willie's sister tells his mother she has dreamed of Willie's drowning. Willie's mother tears her hair. She and his uncle ask was there no one to save him? Willie's funeral was a grand sight.

Tom Munnelly collected at least thirteen versions of the song during the early years of his collecting career, from Travellers for the most part. Singers also gave Tom titles such as 'The Lakes of Sheelin' or 'The Lake of Shellin'. Collectors with the Irish Folklore Commission also collected versions of the ballad in the 1930s, 1940s, and 1950s, including a text collected by Seán Ó Cróinín from his mother, the well-known singer, Elizabeth ('Bess') Cronin in County Cork.

There was a boy from Gort and he was gone harvesting to the County Tipperary and it was in the time of the Famine. His mother was in the workhouse in Gort the time he started for Tipperary.

He was only about a week working when he had a dream that his mother was dead. 'Give me my money,' he says, 'and let me home. I had a dream that my mother is dead.' 'No', says the man, 'you'll wait another while.'

The second night the boy had a dream again that his mother was dead and when he asked the boss to let him home, he wouldn't. Begor, he dreamed again the third night that she was dead, and nothing could keep him. Home he went to Gort and when he went to enquire at the workhouse they told him that she was buried in Bully's Acre. The boy went as far as Bully's Acre and when he searched about he found his mother moaning. He brought her home with him and she lived for years afterwards.

Told by Johnny Murphy (88), Acus, Feakle, County Clare to Seán Ó Flannagáin, 4.11.1937. Johnny heard it from his parents in 1877. They were then aged fifty. (NFC 433:68-70)

'Third time lucky' is a phrase used so commonly that no particular heed is paid to it. In the preceding account, the fact that the boy had the same dream three times in succession motivated him to act in the third instance. In Ireland, at a time of severe famine and associated cholera and other diseases, the fear of being buried alive must have been very real. The dramatic effect of the narration is heightened by the knowledge that Jonny Murphy's parents had firsthand experience of the Famine.

The Otherworld Music & Song from Irish Tradition

Port na bPúcaí [The Tune of the Fairies]

lilted by Muiris Ó Dálaigh

Is é m'athair a thóg é, dtuigeas tú. Scéal púcaí is ea é. Bhí sé thiar in Inis Mhic Aoibhleáin agus am éigin den lá nó den oíche do chuala sé an ghuth ag seimint an phort seo agus thóg sé síos é. Thóg sé ina cheann é. Bhuel is é an chuma théadh sí …

Is iomaí plé a bhíonn ar siúl faoi fhoinsí port agus ceoil agus faoina n-ainmneacha agus a n-ainmniú. Samhlaítear an port seo le Corca Dhuibhne agus le hInis Mhic Aoibhleáin go háirithe. Tugtar 'Caoineadh na bhFairies' nó 'Caoineadh na Sióg' air seo chomh maith. De réir an tseanchais is ceol draíochta nó ceol sí atá ann. Tá focail ag dul leis an bport agus bhailigh Ciarán Mac Mathúna leagan de na focail ó Thomás Ó Dálaigh, deartháir Mhuiris. Faoi mar atá ráite ag Pádraig Ua Maoileoin, ní ró-mhaith a théann na focail leis an bport, cé go bhfuil na focail ceangailte go dlúth leis na sióga agus leis an tuairim gur ó bhean sí a tháinig an port:

*Is bean ón slua sí mé a tháinig thar toinn,
Is gur goideadh san oíche mé tamall
thar lear,
Is go bhfuilim sa ríocht faoi gheasa mná sí.
Is ní bhead ar an saol seo go nglaofaidh
an coileach.*

Sa leabhar 'The Western Island or The Great Blasket' thug Robin Flower cuntas ar an gcaoi ar thóg duine ón Oileán an port seo. Rinne sé cur síos ar an dlúthcheangal ag domhan na siógaí le domhan an duine agus ar thábhacht an cheoil sa gcomhthéacs seo.

Is iomaí taifeadadh den phort seo ann agus is iondúil gur mar fhonn mall a sheinntear é, ach sa leagan ag Dálaigh tá rithim sean válsa leis.

B'as Inis Mhic Aoibhleáin, Muiris Ó Dálaigh, 'Dálaigh' ó thús. Cailleadh a thuismitheoirí agus é an-óg agus tháinig sé féin agus a dheartháireacha chun cónaithe go dtí an mórthír. Choinnigh sé dlúththeagmháil le muintir an Bhlascaoid i gcónaí.

Inis Mhic
Aoibhleáin,
County Kerry,
2012.

The Otherworld Music & Song from Irish Tradition

Ba mhinic é ag dul ar cuairt go dtí an tOileán, áit a mbíodh sé ag seinm cheoil ar an mbosca, ag fonnadóireacht agus ag damhsa. Chaith sé cuid mhór dá shaoil i mBaile na Rátha, Dún Chaoin. Ba mhinic an veidhleadóir Seáinín Mhicil Ó Súilleabháin, iar-Bhlascaodach eile in éineacht leis agus iad ag ceol. Fuair sé bás sa bhliain 1990 agus é ceithre scór bliain d'aois.

Ba é Leo Corduff (1929-1992) an rinne an taifeadadh seo i 1963. Bhí Leo ina bhailitheoir béaloidis agus i mbun na cartlainne fuaime. Thosaigh sé ag obair do Choimisiún Béaloideasa Éireann i lár na gcaogaidí. B'as Ros Dumhach Leo ó dhúchas áit ar bhailigh a athair Michael cuid mhór ábhar don Choimisiún. Mar oifigeach taifeadta bhailigh Leo ábhar ó cheann ceann na tíre atá anois ina bhunchloch sa chartlann fuaime, Cnuasach Bhéaloideas Éireann.

The Tune of the Fairies

My father got it you know. It is a story about the fairies. He was over in Inis Mhic Aoibhleáin and some time during the day or night he heard a voice making this tune and he noted it.
He remembered it.
Well, this is how it went...

Tunes, their origins and nomenclature are frequently a subject for discussion. This tune is associated with Corca Dhuibhne and especially with Inis Mhic Aoibhleáin in west Kerry. It is also called 'Caoineadh na bhFairies' or 'Caoineadh na Sióg' (The Fairies' Lament). Oral tradition says it is magical or fairy music. There are words to accompany the tune and Ciarán Mac Mathúna collected a version of the words from Tomás Ó Dálaigh, a brother of Muiris. The Corca Dhuibhne author, Pádraig Ua Maoileoin, has observed that the words do not sit very well with the tune. The text is written from the perspective of a fairy woman.

> I am a fairy woman,
> who has come across the sea,
> I was taken away during the night
> to spend some time abroad,
> I am in this kingdom by the grace
> of a fairy woman,
> I will be on this earth until the cock crows.

In the book *The Western Island or The Great Blasket* Robin Flower described how an islandman came by this tune. In this account we have a perceptive account of the intersection of the fairy world with the mortal world and of the importance of music in this regard:

> The fairies, they say are not immortal, they, too, know death, and the music that went over the house on the island that night was a lament for one of the fairy host that had died and was carried to this island for burial. (Flower 1944,116)

Muiris Ó Dálaigh - better known as 'Dálaigh' - was originally from Inis Mhic Aoibhleáin. His parents died when he was very young and he and his brothers went to live on the mainland. He remained in constant contact with the community of The Great Blasket where he was a frequent visitor. He played music on the accordion, sang and danced. He lived for much of his life in Baile na Rátha, Dún Chaoin, County Kerry. Dálaigh and the fiddle player and former Blasket Islander, Seáinín Mhicil Ó Súilleabháin were often heard playing music together. Numerous recordings of 'Port na bPúcaí' have been made where it is played as a slow air. In this recording, however, Dálaigh's version is closer to waltz-tempo. Dálaigh died in 1990 at eighty years of age.

Muiris Ó Dálaigh

Leo Corduff (1929-1992) made this recording in 1963. He began working for the Irish Folklore Commission in the mid-1950s. Leo was a native of Ros Dumhach in County Mayo where his father, Michael, collected a great deal of material for the Irish Folklore Commission. As sound-recording officer, Leo travelled throughout Ireland and his recordings today form a cornerstone of the sound archive at the National Folklore Collection.

The inherent dangers of engaging with the fairies or their music are illustrated by Mícheál Ó Súilleabháin here. Verbs such as 'taken', 'swept' or 'overlooked', often used to describe fairy activity, communicate the sense of a malevolent force and signify a fear of abduction and loss.

There is a big fort in Derrygorman called Lismore. One day there was a woman going along the road and she heard the lovely music. The woman was wondering where the music was coming from and at last she noticed that the music came out of the fort. She went home and in a few weeks she got sick and died. People say so. She was 'swept'.

Told by Mícheál Ó Súilleabháin (76), Annascaul, County Kerry to Dónall Ó Gormáin, 14.12.1920. (NFC 744:81)

Leo Corduff with Traveller children, County Mayo, 1958.

The Otherworld *Music & Song from Irish Tradition*

Réidhchnoc Mná Duibhe
[The Smooth Hill of the Dark Woman]

sung by Pádraig Ó Cearnaigh

Is fada mise ar buaireamh ag cur tuairisc mo ghrá,
Trí ghleanntán dubhach uaigneach do mo ruagairt chun fáin,
A samhail siúd ní bhfuaireas cé gur chuardaíos a lán,
Ó chaisibh na tuaithe go dtí bruachleac na Má.

Do casadh mo ghrá liom is ba náireach liom gan suí,
Do leagas mo láimh ar a bráid is ar a croí,
Is é a dúirt sí: 'Anois fág mé mar ní shamhail duit mé,
Mar is bean dubhach ar an bhfán mé do ráingigh i do shlí.'

'Más "bean dubhach ar an bhfán mé do ráingigh i do shlí,"
Suigh anseo láimh liom is tabhair dúshlán faoi gach buíon,
An tú maighdean mhánla na dtáithíní buí,
Nó an tú an stuairín mhilis, mhánla a sciob Páras ón dTraoi?'

'Ní haon ní den méid sin, mise féin dá ndúraís,
Ach cailín ciúin Gaelach ón dtaobh eile thíos,
Níor shíneas-sa riamh mo thaobh deas le haon fhear san ríocht,
Agus tóg díom do ghéaga, táim déanach óm' buíon.'

Nuair do thógas mo ghéaga dá caol choimín síos,
Ba ghile ar a taobh í ná an sneachta ar an gcraoibh,
An iad sluaite Chnoc Bhréanainn do ráingigh i mo lín,
Agus uaimse gur léim sí go dtí Réidhchnoc Mná Duibhe.

Ba ghile í ná an sneachta is ná an t-airgead bán,
Ba ghile í ná an fhaoileann ar líonloch ar snámh,
Ba bhreá deas iad a cuacha ina truapall léi síos,
Ar gach taobh dá guailne is iad ag luascadh le gaoth.

Pádraig Ó Cearnaigh

The Otherworld *Music & Song from Irish Tradition*

Sa tradisiún béil, samhlaítear áiteacha faoi leith mar áit chónaithe ag an lucht sí agus pearsana osnádúrtha.

Tá leagan den amhrán seo foilsithe in 'The Poets and Poetry of Munster' ag John O'Daly, áit a bhfuil aistriúchán déanta ag James Clarence Mangan air. Tugtar síos ann, gur fear darbh ainm Seoirse Robart a chum. Is minic 'Réidhchnoc Mná Sí' mar theideal ar an amhrán lena mínítear na tagairtí ann don mbuíon, nó don slua sí. De réir mar atá san amhrán anseo, is léir gur bean atá i gceist a d'éalaigh ón slua sí ar feadh tamaill, a casadh ar an bhfile agus gur thit sé i ngrá léi. Buaileann eagla í go bhfuil na sióga ag teacht ar a tóir le hí a thabhairt ar ais leo agus imíonn sí de léim go dtí Réidhchnoc Mná Duibhe, áit ar ndóigh a bhfuil cónaí ar an slua sí. Tugtar blas áitiúil don leagan den amhrán faoi mar a chasann Pádraig Ó Cearnaigh é, nuair a deirtear ann gur ó Chnoc Bhréanainn anuas atá an slua sí ag teacht ar thóir na mná. Is iondúil i leaganacha eile den amhrán gur ó Chnoc Gréine i Luimneach atá na sióga ag teacht chuici. Tá an t-amhrán grá seo neamhchoitianta sa mhéid go bhfuil tréithe den eachtra nó den scéal ann, seachas mothúcháin amháin á gcur i lathair.

Ón mBlascaod Mór ab ea Pádraig Sheáisí Ó Cearnaigh áit ar chaith sé cuid mhór dá shaol. Tháinig sé féin, Cáit, a bhean chéile agus a gclann chun na míntíre go Muiríoch, i gCorca Dhuibhne i 1948. Bhí an-réimse amhrán aige a fuair sé den chuid is mó ó mhuintir an Oileáin. Iascaire ab ea é. Fuair sé bás sa bhliain 1986. Tá an leagan seo ag Pádraig le cloisteáil ar an dlúthdhiosca Beauty an Oileáin *a foilsíodh i 1992. Ba iad Radió Éireann a rinne an leagan seo a thaifeadadh i 1958.*

The Smooth Hill of the Dark Woman

A version of this love-song is published in '*The Poets and Poetry of Munster*' by John O'Daly and translated there by James Clarence Mangan. The author's name is given there as Seoirse Robart or George Roberts. The song is frequently called 'Réidhchnoc Mná Sí' or 'The Dark Fairy Rath' as translated by Mangan. The woman, evidently, has escaped from the fairies for a short while, during which time the poet meets her and falls in love with her. She fears that she has outstayed her sojourn in the mortal world and that the fairy host will come to fetch her back, so she swiftly leaps back to 'Réidhchnoc Mná Duibhe', where the fairies live. The song as sung by Pádraig Ó

Cearnaigh has a local flavour as here the fairies are said to come from Cnoc Bhréanainn in the Dingle peninsula in Kerry rather than from Cnoc Gréine (The Hill of the Sun) in Limerick which is referred to in most other versions of the song. This love-song is somewhat unusual in the Irish-language song tradition as it contains narrative traits along with intense expression of emotions.

**I have been a long time searching
for my beloved
Wandering through dark lonely glens
sending me astray,
I did not find her like although I searched
far and wide,
From the streams of the countryside
to brink of the River Maigue.**

**I met my love and was drawn to sit by her,
I placed my hand on her breast and on
her heart,
She said:
'Now leave me because I am not for you
Because I am a sorrowful woman, astray,
whom you happened to meet.'**

**'If you are a sorrowing woman astray
whom I happened to meet,
Sit here beside me and challenge every host,
Are you the gentle girl of the yellow curls
Or are you the sweet, gentle handsome
woman Paris stole from Troy?'**

**'I am none of those whom you mentioned,
But a quiet Irish girl from down the other side,
I never lay with any man alive,
And rise up from me;
I am late in my return to the host.'**

**When I rose up from her slender form,
Her form was brighter than the snow
on the branch,
Was it the hosts of Cnoc Bhréanainn
that I caught in the net,
And she darted from me to the
Smooth Hill of the Dark Woman.**

**She was brighter than the snow and
than bright money,
She was brighter than the gull swimming
on the full lake,
Her ringlets hanging down from her
were beautiful
On both sides of her shoulders as they
swayed with the breeze.**

Pádraig Sheáisí Ó Cearnaigh was born on the Great Blasket Island and lived there most of his life. He was a fisherman who had a wide repertoire of songs, which he learned, for the most part on the island. In 1948, Pádraig went to live with Cáit, his wife and their family in Muiríoch, Corca Dhuibhne, where he died in 1986. This recording was made by Radió Éireann in 1958 and also appeared on the compact disc *Beauty an Oileáin* published in 1992.

In the townland of Upper Doirín Parish of Áth an tSléibhe there is a mound of earth about forty feet high, covering about half an acre. …One morning early a man named John Hanrahan heard horses going out of the hill and he could hear the saddles creaking as if they were new. He heard the horses galloping up the fields, but he could not see anything even though the morning was bright.

Another morning a man named Jack Casey was out when the sun was rising, and when he looked at the 'cnocán' he saw it all covered with a big castle that looked like gold shining in the sun but when he went near it he only saw the 'cnocán' the same as it always was.

Collected by Caoimhín Ó Danachair, December 1934 in his native district Athea, County Limerick. (NFC 96:147-150)

This is a rich and vivid description of the sounds of fairy horses riding out. In oral tradition, the fairies, for the most part, behave in the manner of humans. Both parts of the narration accentuate the association of otherworldly happenings on the top of mounds or hills.

Fairy mound at Lattin, County Tipperary.

Pilib Séimh Ó Fathaigh

sung by Ciarán Ó Gealbháin

Aréir agus mé ag machnamh ar mhaoilinn an leasa,
Cé chífinn chugam ag tarraingt ach an tsíbhruinneall óg,
A raibh a bratchumha léi go talamh, a géaga léi ar leathadh,
Is a cuacha buí gan chasadh ag titim léi go feor.
D'fhiosraíosa féineach den ainnir cér díobh í nó a hainm:
'An tú síbhean na Craige, ríon Airt nó Mór?
Nó Anna Chaomh Nic Gearailt, géag dhlúth dár gcaraid,
Atá ag éileamh an mharcaigh sa mBuí-Chnoc fé bhrón?'

Shuigh taobh liom an ainnir, a haolchrobh mar an eala,
An réiltean gan ghangaid do b'áille ar bith snó.
'A shéimh fhir a labhair', ag géarghol is ag ceasnaighil,
'Réifidh mé do gheasa ach suímis go fóill.
Is mé Anna Chaomh Nic Gearailt ó Dhún Aolta na Seabhac,
Mar a bhfuil tréanfhuil ag caismirt go dian ann as mo dheoidh;
Táim traochta le tamall ó bheith ag éileamh bhur mairbh,
Is é Pilib séimh ceart Ó Fathaigh fáth mo dhobróin.'

Mo léan agus mo thuirse! An séimh-fhear gan fuinneamh,
'bheith daorsnoite i dtinneas is i bhfaoilteacha bróin,
Nó arbh fhéidir go gcuirfeadh an séithleach ortsa an cluiche?
Glaoigh feasta ar Mhic Mhuire is ar Bhanríon na hÓighe.
Beidh do chéile agus do linbh ag géarghol go connail,
I d'éileamhsa, a Philib, is tú sínte gan treoir;
Is má théann ort san imirt, dein liom ionad coinne,
Is raghaidh mé i d'fhéachaint Lá 'l Muire go Buí-Chnoc na sló.

Is méin liomsa feasta ar do ghaoltasa labhairt,
A shéimhfhir gan ghangaid, a shíolraigh ón bpór;
Gréagaigh is Craithigh is na Paoraigh ab fhearra,
Lucht éigse do labhairt, lucht saghad agus treon.
Níl aon díobh ina mbeathaidh a réifeadh ár ngeasa,
Glaoite as diaidh d'ainmse sa tír úd id' dheoidh,
Ó shéanais do charaid ag dul faoi bhéil lice i nglasaibh,
Mar a chuaigh Phoebus fá scamall sa mBuí-Chnoc faoi bhrón.

The Otherworld *Music & Song from Irish Tradition*

Ba é Tomás Mac Craith a chum an caoineadh seo san 18ú haois. Mac deirféar dó a phós duine de mhuintir Fhathaigh ba ea Pilib agus mhair an file in aon tíos leo le linn do Philib a bheith ag fás aníos. Tugadh an Craitheach abhaile ón Róimh, de réir dealraimh, áit go raibh sé ina ábhar sagart, nuair a cuireadh muintir Mhic Craith as seilbh i gCurrach na Slaodaí, Sliabh gCua – ní raibh ar a gcumas na táillí a dhíol dó ina dhiaidh sin.

Badhbh, nó bean-sí, ba ea Anna Chaomh a bhí luaite go mór leis na Gearaltaigh (na Gréagaigh san amhrán) agus ba iad na Craithigh saighdiúirí tuarastal na nGearaltach sa cheantar de réir an tseanchais. De réir tuairiscí áirithe, duine de Ghearaltaigh na Scairte, teaghlach mór a bhí i Sliabh gCua ba ea Anna Chaomh agus thug na daoine maithe leo í go Dún Aill de réir na gcuntas seo. Rinneadh dlúthcheangal i bhfad siar sa traidisiún Gaelach idir Anna nó Áine (bandia sa mhiotaseolaíocht is bean sí an bhéaloidis) agus Gearaltaigh Dheasmhumhan, na taoisigh Normannacha a tháinig isteach ón iasacht. Ní deacair an nasc seo idir Áine agus na Gearaltaigh a dhéanamh amach: níl ach dhá mhíle slí idir Chnoc Áine i gContae Luimní, an áit is suntasaí atá

luaite léi sa mhiotaseolaíocht, agus Loch Gair, áit a raibh tigh túir ag na Gearaltaigh chomh fada siar leis an tríú céad déag. Ainm mór sa bhéaloideas agus sa litríocht is ea 'Gearóid Iarla' Mac Gearailt (1338-1398), tríú hiarla Dheasmhumhan. Tá sé ráite sa bhéaloideas gurbh í an bhandia Áine a mháthair-sean, mar gur bheir a athair uirthi, lá, ag cíoradh a cuid gruaige ar bhruach abhainn na Camóige. Amhrán é 'Pilib Séimh Ó Fathaigh' a bhíodh le clos go minic ag Labhrás Ó Cadhla ó Scairt na Draighní i gceantar Shliabh gCua. Tá cuntas iomlán ar an amhrán agus a stair in Ó Gealbháin 2006.

De bhunadh an tSeanphobail i nGaeltacht na nDéise é Ciarán Ó Gealbháin mar a bhfuil cónaí fós air. Iarbhall den ghrúpa ceoil Danú, ceoltóir agus amhránaí is ea é a chuireann suim fé leith i dtraidisiún amhránaíochta na nDéise. Bhí tionchar nach beag ag amhránaithe a cheantair féin ar Chiarán ag fás aníos dó, Séamus Mac Craith agus Nioclás Tóibín ina measc, agus is mó amhrán a d'fhoghlaim sé ó dheirfiúr Nioclás, Eibhlís Tóibín Bean de Paor, i mBarr na Stuac sa Seanphobal. Tá céim sa Ghaeilge agus sa Léann Dúchais bainte aige ó Choláiste na hOllscoile Corcaigh, áit a bhfuil sé ag

Lough Gur,
County Limerick,
2012.

The Otherworld *Music & Song from Irish Tradition*

léachtóireacht agus i mbun tráchtas dochtúireachta i Roinn an Bhéaloidis faoi láthair.

Gentle Pilib Ó Fathaigh

This lament was composed by Tomás Mac Craith in the eighteenth century. Pilib was a son of the poet's sister who was married to an Ó Fathaigh. MacCraith was living in the same house as them while Pilib was a child Following their eviction from their home in Sliabh gCua, in County Waterford the MacCraith family were unable to pay the seminary fees in Rome where Tomás had commenced his study for the priesthood. He was obliged to return home.

Anna Caomh was a woman of the fairy host in the district and was closely identified with the Mac Gearailt family (the Greeks [Gréagaigh] in the song). According to oral tradition, the Mac Craiths were paid soldiers of the Mac Gearailt family in the locality.

Some accounts have it that Anna was one of the Gearaltaigh from An Scairt, a noble family that resided in Sliabh gCua and she was abducted by the fairies to Dún Aill. In early Irish tradition, a close connection existed between Anna or Áine (the goddess of mythology and the fairy woman of folk tradition) and the Gearaltaigh of Desmond, the Norman lords who came from abroad. This connection between Áine and the Gearaltaigh is easily explained. There are only two miles between Cnoc Áine in County Limerick, the most renowned place associated with her in mythology and Loch Gur where the Gearaltaigh owned a tower house as early as the thirteenth century. 'Gearóid Iarla'or 'Gerald the Rhymer' (Fitzgerald) (1338-1398) is a famous name in folklore and in literature. He was the third earl of Desmond. Oral tradition claims that the goddess Áine was his mother, as his father found her one day combing her hair on the edge of the river Camóg. Labhrás Ó Cadhla from Scairt na Draighní in Sliabh gCua often sang this song.

Last night as I reflected on top
of the fairy mound,
I saw coming towards me an
enchanting young fairy woman,
Her mourning shroud engulfed her,
her arms were outspread,

And her straight golden hair flowed
to the ground.
I asked the beautiful girl who she was
or what was her name:
'Are you the fairy woman of An Chraig,
the queen of Airt or Mór?
Or gentle Anna Nic Gearailt,
a true support of our friends,
Asking for the rider who lies sorrowful
in the Fair Hill?'

The young woman sat beside me,
her fair hand was like a swan,
This guileless lady had the most
beautiful complexion.
'Gentle man who has spoken',
she lamented and complained,
'I will release the spell, but let us sit awhile.
I am gentle Anna Nic Gearailt from
Dún Aolta na Seabhac,
Where warriors of noble blood are
in conflict about me,
I am wearied for a while from demanding
your dead,
Pilib Séimh Ó Fathaigh,
is the cause of my woe.'

My sorrow and my heartbreak!
The gentle man without vigour,
That he is worn down by illness and
great sorrow,
Or is it possible that the weakling
will betray you?
Henceforth, invoke Our Lady, the Virgin Mary.
Your partner and your child will lament quietly,
Asking for you, Pilib, where you are laid low,
And if you lose the game, arrange to meet me,
And I will go to see you to the Fair Hill of the
host on Our Lady's feast day.

I would like to speak of your relations,
Gentle, honest man, descended from
the ancestry of
Gréagaigh and Craithigh and
the best Paoraigh,
Those with great power of word,
of arrows and of strength.
None who are living can release our spell,
Called after you by name in that country,
Since you betrayed your friend who
is buried in the ground,
As Phoebus went sorrowfully into the Fair Hill.

Ciarán Ó Gealbháin is from An Seanphobal in the Déise Gaeltacht where he still lives today. A former member of the music group 'Danú', he is a musician and singer with a special interest in the singing tradition of the Déise. In his youth, he was very much influenced by well-known singers in the locality, including Séamus Mac Craith and Nioclás Tóibín, and he learned a number of songs from Nioclás sister, Eibhlís Tóibín Bean de Paor, in Barr na Stuac. Ciarán studied Irish and Folklore at University College Cork where he is currently lecturing in the Department of Folklore and Ethnology.

Bhí fear ann fadó agus bhí sé pósta. Thóg na daoine maithe a bhean a mealladh uaidh agus bhí brón mór air. Dúirt sé leis féin go rachadh sé ar a tóir agus amach leis. Bhí sé ag smaoineamh go mb'fhéidir gur suas go Cnoc Meá a thóg siad an bhean agus dúirt sé leis [féin] go mbainfeadh sé an cnoc agus nuair a d'fheicfeadh siad eisean go mb'fhéidir go ligfeadh siad an bhean amach sula mbeadh sé bainte ar fad. Thosaigh sé air ag obair agus tar éis cúpla lá lig siad an bhean amach mar bhí faitíos orthu go millfeadh sé an cnoc. Chuaigh sé a chodladh gach oíche ann nuair a bhí sé ag baint, agus an áit a bhí sé ina chodladh tá leac ann agus is é an t-ainm a thugtar air timpeall na háite seo 'Leac Dháibhí'.

John Flanagan (50), Cave, Caherlistrane, Contae na Gaillimhe a fuair óna athair. (CBÉ 79: 205)

Long ago there lived a man and he was married. The good people enticed his wife away from him and he was very sad. He said to himself he would go in search of her and off he went. He was thinking they might have taken her up to Cnoc Meá and he said to himself that he would dig the hill and when they would see him they might let his wife out before it would be completely dug. He began working and after a few days they let his wife out because they were afraid he would destroy the hill. He slept there every night when he was digging and it is called 'Leac Dháibhí' 'Dáibhí's Stone' around here.

Told by John Flanagan (50), Cave, Caherlistrane, County Galway. He heard it from his father. (NFC 79:205)

Ways of duping or deceiving the fairies were part and parcel of life and in the preceding account the threat of destruction of one of their most illustrious residences, that of Cnoc Meá, near Tuam in County Galway, forces them to restore to her husband a mortal woman they have stolen.

The Otherworld Music & Song from Irish Tradition

Ciarán Ó Gealbháin

Tiúin an Phíobaire Sí [The Tune of the Fairy Piper]

lilted by Máire Ní Bheirn

Rinne siad amach ansin gur anuas as an ard i gcúl an tí a tháinig sé agus gur píobaire sí a bhí ann – ach bhí seo go breá chomh maith agus sheinn sé agus is í an tiúin a sheinn sé …

Tá cuid mhór sa seanchas faoi cheoltóirí, go háirithe píobairí, ón saol eile a tháinig i measc na ndaoine agus a sheinn ceol agus ba mhinic iad imithe as amharc chomh tobann céanna is a tháinig siad. Sa mbliain 1974 rinne Máire cur síos ar an bpíobaire sí do Mhícheál Ó Domhnaill sula dtug sí 'Tiúin an Phíobaire Sí' uaithi agus í ag déanamh portaireacht bhéil:

Pósadh cailín ins an tseanam i dteach thuas anseo thuas i gcúl an aird ansin agus bhíodh sé mall nuair a phóstaí na lánúnacha san am sin tráthnóna agus ar ndóigh bhíodh sé anonn go maith san oíche nuair a ghabhfadh siad abhaile. Bhíodh sé an-doiligh na fir a fháil abhaile. Bhíodh siad ag ól braonacha is

tháinig siad sa deireadh agus cuireadh fhad leis an chuid iad a bhí réidh fá na gcoinne. Agus anois nuair a bhí an ceathrú round thíos insa tseomra ag déanamh a gcuid, tháinig buachaill deas isteach ar an doras cúl, buachaill dóighiúil rua, agus culaith an-deas gorm air agus péire píoba leis faoina ascaill. Shuigh sé ar cheann stóil a bhí síos i dtaobh an tí agus tharraing sé na píob agus chuaigh sé a sheinm. Sheinn sé anois go maidin an tiúin amháin agus bhí siad uilig ag damhsa agus bhí oíche an-mhaith acu agus níor chuir duine ar bith aon suim ann go fóill. Bhí siad uilig, braon ólta acu, agus bhí siad ag damhsa agus bhí siad an-suáilceach san oíche – bhí oíche an-mhaith acu –agus nuair a tháinig solas an lae, nó roimhe sholas an lae, d'imigh sé amach ar an doras chéanna a dtáinig sé isteach as agus níor chreathnaigh cuid acu ar chor ar bith é – tuilleadh a chonaic gabháil amach é agus mar sin – ach nuair a tháinig as an lá chuaigh siad a chaint air, an

The Otherworld *Music & Song from Irish Tradition*

Left to right: Seán Mac Briartaigh (John Tamaí), Conall Ó Beirn (Con John an Bheirnigh), Seán Mac Briartaigh (John Mhánais), Pádraig Ó Cuinneagáin (Pat Eoin), Séamas Ó hEochaidh (Jimi Phaidí), Peadar Ó Beirn (Peadar Johnny Johndie) Pádraig Ó Beirn (young boy), 1935.

bunadh a bhí ansin an t-am ar smaoitigh siad air – chuaigh siad amach – bhí mórán lucht siúil ar a gcois ins an am sin – chuaigh siad amach fríd na tithe a stopfadh siad iontu – agus ní raibh aon duine acu insan áit an oíche seo – aon duine amháin acu insan áit.

Thugtaí 'Máire an Ghréasaí' ar Mháire Ní Bheirn, Bealach Bhun Ghlas, An Charraig.
Bhí cáil an cheoil agus an spraoi ar chlann Johnny Johndie Ó Beirn – Máire, Peadar agus Condy (Conall). Teach mór cuartaíochta agus oícheanta airneáin, ceoil agus damhsa a bhí ann. Tá an teach ann i gcónaí. Tógadh an teach ar idirthalamh idir dhá bhaile fearainn, Iomaire Mhuireanáin agus An Cheapach Uachtarach. Fuair Máire bás i 1976 nuair a bhí sí 78 mbliain d'aois.

Sa bhliain 1974 chaith Mícheál Ó Domhnaill (1951-2006) ó Aibreán go Lúnasa ag obair do Rannóg an Cheoil, Roinn Bhéaloideas Éireann, An Coláiste Ollscoile, Baile Átha Cliath (Cnuasach Bhéaloideas Éireann anois). Ba é Breandán Breathnach a bhí ina stiúrthóir ag an mbailitheoir óg. Le linn na tréimhse seo, bhailigh Mícheál na céadta amhrán, portaireacht bhéil agus seanchas i gContae Dhún na nGall. Seo a leanas dhá shliocht ó dhialann Mhíchíl, samhradh 1974, faoi Mháire Johnny Johndie:

Mícheál
Ó Domhnaill

Céadaoin 3 Iúil

Chas mé le Máire Beirn (Máire Johnny Johndie) inniu. Lá caidheach a bhí ann agus fliuchadh arís mé. Seanbhean ceithre scór bliain í – í beag, tanaí agus gruaig dhubh uirthi. Caithfidh gur ceoltóir iontach a bhí inti nuair a bhí sí óg – fiú amháin inniu tá guth breá soiléir aici. Tá eagla orm go bhfuil an chuid is mó dá cuid ceoil dearmadta aici, ach tá cúpla rud fágtha go fóill aici. Rachaidh mé aici arís gan mhoill.

Céadaoin 10 Iúil

Chuaigh mé ar ais ag Mary Beirn (Teileann) inniu, agus cheol sí cúpla amhrán dom. Tá dúil mhór aici i bhfíon agus i snaoisín. Chonacthas dom go raibh stíl iontach deas portaíocht aici (cf.....Tiúin an Phíobaire).

Tugtar 'The Heathery Cruach' agus 'John Mhósaí McGinley's Reel' freisin ar an ríl 'Tiúin an Phíobaire Sí' agus thaifeadaigh an grúpa Altan é. Thaifeadaigh an fidléir ó Bhaile Átha Cliath, James Kelly é agus tharlódh gur chuala seisean ag John Doherty é. Ba chara é John Doherty le hathair James, John Kelly, fidléir agus seinnteoir ar an gconsairtín.

The Tune of the Fairy Piper

They made out then that he had come down from the hill behind the house and that he was a fairy piper – but that was fine as he had played so wonderfully and this is the tune he played.

There is a great deal of lore about musicians, especially pipers, from the Otherworld, who suddenly and mysteriously appeared among mortals and played music. They would then disappear just as quickly. Máire Ní Bheirn described the fairy piper in the account she gave Mícheál Ó Domhnaill in 1974 before lilting 'Tiúin an Phíobaire Sí' ('The Tune of the Fairy Piper').

The Otherworld Music & Song from Irish Tradition

The Otherworld *Music & Song from Irish Tradition*

Long ago a girl married in a house up here behind that height and couples married later in the day back then, and of course it was quite late in the evening when they went home. It was very hard to get the men to go home. They used to drink some and in the end they came and they were directed to the food that had been prepared for them. And when the fourth round was eating in the room, a nice young man came in the back door, a handsome redhaired lad, with a fine blue suit and a set of pipes under his arm. He sat up on a stool, which was along the side of the house and drew out the pipes and began to play. From then until morning he played the same tune and they were all dancing and they had a great night and no one paid any heed to him. They were all a bit merry, and they were dancing and they were very happy in the night – they had a great night – and at daybreak, or before daybreak, he went out the same door he had come in and none of them missed him at all – some saw him go and so on – but when day came and they were talking about him, those who were there at the time and thought of him – they went out – there were many travelling folk about then – they went to search the houses where they used to stay and none of them had one staying that night, none of them in the district.

Máire Ní Bheirn, Bealach Bhun Ghlas, An Charraig was known as 'Máire an Ghréasaí'. Johnny Johndie Ó Beirn's family – Máire, Peadar and Condy – were known for their music and singing. Their house was renowned as a house for visiting and for nights of entertainment, music and dancing. The house is still standing. It was built on 'no-man's land' between two townlands – Iomaire Mhuireanáin and An Cheapach Uachtarach. Máire died in 1976 aged 78.

The National Folklore Collection now houses the fieldwork and recordings made by Mícheál Ó Domhnaill (1951-2006) in 1974 in Donegal. Mícheál had been engaged by Brendán Breathnach to collect in Donegal - a place he knew well and to which he had close family ties. During this time he collected hundreds of songs, lilting and lore in Irish and English. The following is a translation of two extracts from Mícheál's diary, summer 1974, in relation to Máire Johnny Johndie:

Wednesday 3 July

I met Máire Beirn (Máire Johnny Johndie) today. It was a terrible day and I was wet again. She is an old woman eighty years of age – small, thin with black hair. She must have been a great singer when she was young. She still has a fine, clear voice. I fear she has forgotten most of her songs but she still remembers a few things. I will visit her again without delay.

Wednesday 10 July

I went back to Mary Beirn (Teileann) today and she sang a few songs for me. She is very fond of wine and of snuff. I think she has an extremely nice lilting style. (cf…..Tiúin an Phíobaire).

The reel 'Tiúin an Phíobaire Sí' is also known as 'The Heathery Cruach' and 'John Mhósaí McGinley's Reel' and was recorded by the group Altan. It was also recorded by Dublin fiddle player James Kelly who may have heard it from John Doherty, a friend and contemporary of his father, fiddle and concertina player, John Kelly.

An bunadh seo a bhíodh ar shiúl ag scibireacht ar an abhainn, is minic a chluineadh siad rudaí iontacha eadar meán oíche is lá. Chuala mé fear acu a rá go raibh sé thíos acu ag an abhainn go han-luath ar maidin, agus chuala sé an píobaire a ba deise a chuala sé ariamh. Sheas sé ag éisteacht leis, agus chonaictheas dó nach gcuala sé ceol ar bith ariamh ina shaol a ba bhinne ná an rud a bhí sé a sheinm. D'imigh an píobaire leis siar a chois na habhna, agus bhí sé ag éisteacht leis go dteachaidh sé trí ná ceathair de mhílte ar shiúl. Scanraigh sé ansin, agus phill sé ar an mbaile, agus ón lá sin go dtí an lá a chuaigh sé i dtalamh, ní theachaidh sé a chóir na habhna go luath ná go mall.

Cathal Ó Baoill (60), Mín an Aoirigh, An Charraig, Contae Dhún na nGall a thug do Sheán Ó hEochaidh, Béaloideas *(1954 [1956]) 78.*

Those who used to go out poaching on the river, they often heard strange sounds between midnight and day. I heard one of them say that he was down by the river very early in the morning, and he heard the finest piper he had ever heard. He stood listening to him, and thought he had never in his life heard music that was as sweet as it. The piper headed off westwards along the river and he followed listening until he had gone three or four miles. He took fright then, and returned home, and from that day until the day he was buried he didn't go near the river early or late.

Told by Cathal Ó Baoill (60), Mín an Aoirigh, An Charraig, County Donegal to Seán Ó hEochaidh, Béaloideas *(1954 [1956]) 78.*

Many otherworld events are said to occur between night and day, at an 'in between' time. The result of this particular event caused the man to mend his ways and to decide he would not poach by the river in future.

Taibhse Chonaill [Conall's Ghost]

played on the fiddle by Rónán Galvin

Bhí seanchas ag Máire Ní Bheirn faoin amhras a bhí ar fhear darbh ainm Conall an Chró Bháin faoi phíobaire neamhshaolta agus an chaoi ar dhéileáil Conall leis. As seo ainm an phoirt 'Taibhse Chonaill' dúirt sí. Seo mar a d'inis Máire an scéal a bhain le hainmniú an phoirt do Sheán Ó hEochaidh sna Faoiligh, 1963:

> *Bhí fear anseo sa tsean-am a dtugadh siad 'Conall an Chró Bháin' air, agus bhí siad ag déanamh poitín ins an am sin. Ach d'imigh triúr acu siar oíche amháin fhad le háit a dtugadh siad Ailt an Mhaoileagáin air. Bhí*

teach thiar ansin acu a mbíodh siad ag obair ann. D'éirigh siad gann ins na soithigh agus tháinig beirt de na fir abhaile fá choinne soithí, agus nuair a bhí siad ar shiúl tháinig píobaire ar Chonall. Is é bhí thiar i dteach na stile, agus chuaigh sé a sheinm tiúin dó. Ba léar le Conall gur drochfhear a bhí ann, agus chuaigh sé ag croitheadh braon beag uisce coisreaca a bhí aige agus a réir is mar bhí Conall ag croitheadh an uisce coisreaca bhí seisean ag daingniú leis an teach agus ag seinm níos fearr. Ach sa deireadh tháinig sé isteach chun tí agus chaith Conall an t-uisce coisreaca isteach i ndabhach uisce a bhí

Poitín-making,
c. 1900.

The Otherworld *Music & Song from Irish Tradition*

i dteach na stile. D'imigh sé amach san am sin agus d'imigh sé síos faoi theach na stile go dtí an fharraige agus dhóigh sé síos roimhis, agus níor fhás a dhath féir ná fraoch ná a dhath ó shin ann. (CBÉ 1641:220-221)

Bhí leagan eile den scéal faoi 'Thaibhse Chonaill' ag Máire agus scríobh Seán Ó hEochaidh é seo uaithi c. 1970. 'An diabhal mar phíobaire' atá tugtha síos mar ainm ar an leagan seo agus é ráite i ndeireadh na hinsinte:

Cá bhith ba chiall dó ba ghnách leis an diabhal a theacht soir an bhunadh seo a bhíodh ag gabháil don phoitín sa tsean-am. B'fhéidir go mbíodh sé ag iarraidh cathaigh a chur orthu agus d'aithníodh siad é i gcónaí mar in áit cosa fir a bhí air péire crúb a bhíodh air mar atá ar bhó! Chuala muid seanchas go leor fada ó shin fá dhaoine a dtáinig sé orthu go luath agus go mall. (CBÉ 1791:436)

I ngeall ar fhiosrú faoi fhonn do dhráma raidió don BBC rinne an píobaire agus an bailitheoir Séamus Mac Aonghusa cóip den fhonn 'Tiúin Thaibhse Chonaill' agus den údar focal ar fhocal mar a fuair sé ó Pheadar Ó Beirn, dearthár Mháire Ní Bheirn, iad. Chuir Mac Aonghusa aistriúchán leis freisin sa mbliain 1945. Bhí leagan den phort ag Mac Aonghusa cheana féin óna athair. Scríobh Mac Aonghusa ina dhialann go ndearna sé fiosrú faoin bport le Colm Ó Lochlainn, an foilsitheoir a raibh Mac Aonghusa ag obair dó roimhe sin, agus gur dhúirt seisean leis go mba leagan é de 'The Lady in the Boat'. (Féach CBÉ 1296: 292)

Rugadh agus tógadh Rónán Galvin i gCluain Dolcáin i mBaile Átha Cliath, ach b'as iardheisceart Dhún na nGall a thuismitheoirí. Thosaigh sé ag seinm na fidile agus é ina ghasúr, agus bhí sé faoi anáil stíl agus stór Ghleann Cholm Cille, go mór mór an scothfhidléir, Séamus Ó Beirn (An Beirneach), agus uncail Rónáin, Antain Ó Beirn. Tá sé ag teagasc le blianta fada ag 'Seachtain na bhFidléirí' achan bhliain i nGleann Cholm Cille, agus tá a lán ceardlanna fidile tugtha aige mórán áiteacha, mar shampla, san Ísiltír, sa Fhrainc agus san Eilvéis. Dhírigh a MLitt i mBéaloideas Éireann ar thraidisiún ceoil iardheisceart Dhún na nGall.

Conall's Ghost

On one occasion, Máire Ní Bheirn related that a man called 'Conall an Chró Bháin' doubted the existence of otherworld pipers. This version of the tale provides the background to the tune's title, 'Taibhse Chonaill' ('Conall's Ghost'). Máire gave the story to Seán Ó hEochaidh in February, 1963:

> There was a man here long ago who was known as 'Conall an Chró Bháin' ('Conall of the White Outhouse'), and they used to make poitín at that time. But three of them went off one night to a place they called Ailt an Mhaoileagáin. There was a house in that place where they used to work. They ran out of containers and two of the men returned to fetch containers and while they were gone a piper came to Conall, who was in the still-house and he began to play a tune for him. It was clear to Conall that he was not a good person and he began to shake a little drop of holy water that he had with him, and as Conall was shaking the water, he was coming closer to the house and improving his playing. At last, he came into the house and Conall threw the holy water into a trough of water in the stillhouse. He went out then and went down by the still house to the sea and he burned everything before him and no grass or heather of anything else ever grew there since. And that was the tune he played for Conall. (CBÉ 1641:220-221)

Máire also told another version of the story about 'Taibhse Chonaill' and Seán Ó hEochaidh collected it from her c. 1970. It is called 'An Diabhal mar Phíobaire' ('The Devil as Piper') and the account includes the following:

> Whatever it meant the Devil used to come on those who made poitín in former times. This may have been to encourage them to repent and they would recognise him because instead of the two feet of a man, he had two hooves like the hooves of a cow! We heard a great deal of lore long ago about people he discovered early and late. (CBÉ 1791:436)

The Otherworld Music & Song from Irish Tradition

In response to a request from the BBC in 1945 for a melody suitable for use in a radio play, the collector, Séamus Ennis, transcribed the Teileann tune '*Taibhse Chonaill*' along with the story associated with it as he had received it from Peadar Ó Beirn, a brother of Máire Ní Bheirn. Ennis already had a version of it from his own father and wrote in his diary that he enquired of the publisher, Colm Ó Lochlainn, his former employer, what it was. He told him it was a version of 'The Lady in the Boat'.
(cf. NFC 1296:292)

Rónán Galvin was born and grew up in Clondalkin, Dublin. His parents are from southwest Donegal. As a child, he began to play the fiddle and was greatly influenced by the style and repertoire of Gleann Cholm Cille. He was especially impressed with the playing of James Byrne (An Beirneach) and by his own uncle, Antaine Ó Beirn. For a number of years he has taught at the fiddle week held in early August in Gleann Cholm Cille and has given fiddle workshops in a number of countries including Holland, France and Switzerland. His MLitt. in Irish Folklore focused on the music tradition of southwest Donegal.

Well, fadó shin, bhíodh iascairí Theilinn ar shiúl ins an tsamhradh ag iarraidh bradán. Bhíodh cuid acu an-aonracánach, agus chun deiridh go mór lena gcuid oibre, agus ba mhinic a thigeadh orthu a ghabháil chun an phortaigh i ndiaidh na hoíche fá dhéin cliabh mónadh. Bhí fear as Cruachlann mall ag teacht ó bhád tráthnóna amháin, agus nuair a tháinig sé abhaile ní raibh tine mhónadh sa teach. B'éigean dó breith ar a chliabh agus imeacht chun an phortaigh sular bhlais sé bia ná deoch. Bhí an mhóin thiar i gcúl Chnoc Áine, agus nuair a bhí sé ag gabháil siar ag sáil an chnoic, dar leis gur mhothaigh sé an ceol a ba deise a chuala sé ariamh. Chuaigh sé ar aghaidh giota eile agus ba ghairid a chuaigh sé go dtáinig sé ar phíobaire ina shuí ar leic agus é ag seinm leis. Chaith sé de a chliabh agus rinne sé a sháith damhsa le ceol an phíobaire. Bhí sé ag damhsa gur thuirsigh sé é féin amach. Chuir sé air a chliabh ansin, agus d'imigh leis chun an phortaigh

agus ar a theacht ar ais dó chonaic sé an píobaire ag siúl isteach i dtaoibh an chnoic. Tharraing sé ar an bhall chéanna talaimh sin minic go leor ina dhiaidh sin ach sháraigh air úig ná gaiseach ná foscladh de chineál ar bith fháil i dtaoibh an chnoic.

Conall Ó Beirn (S) (63), Iomaire Mhuireanáin, Teileann, Contae Dhún na nGall a d'inis do Sheán Ó hEochaidh. Béaloideas cf. (1959),10.

Well, long ago, the Teileann fishermen used go in search of salmon in the summer. Some of them were single-handed at home and greatly behind in their work and they often had to go to the bog after nightfall to fetch a basket of turf. A man from Cruachlann was late coming ashore one evening, and when he arrived home there was no turf fire in the house. He had to catch hold of his basket and go to the bog before he could taste any food or drink. The turf was westwards behind Cnoc Áine, and when he was going back at the spur of the hill, he thought he heard the finest music he had ever heard. He went on another bit and he had not gone far when he came upon a piper sitting on a stone playing away. He threw down his basket and danced away to the piper's music. He was dancing until he tired himself out. He put on the basket again and went to the bog and on his return he saw the piper walking into the side of the hill. He often came to the same spot of land often after that but failed to find any cave or cleft or opening of any kind in the side the side of the hill.

Told by Conall Ó Beirn (63), Iomaire Mhuireanáin, Teileann, County Donegal to Seán Ó hEochaidh. Béaloideas (1959),10.

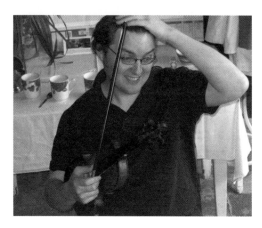

Ronan Galvin

It is easy to imagine a single man returning from a hard day's fishing late on a summer's evening and having to set out to fetch turf in order to prepare food. At a time of slowly declining light the concept of 'in between' springs to mind immediately, a time when mysterious events happen. Conall Ó Beirn's telling of this story not only entices and entertains but offers some insight into the everyday working and living conditions of his people.

Left to right: Cáit Uí Eochaidh, John Tamaí Seáin MacSeáin, Aodh Ó Beirn, Máire Ní Bheirn, Jimí Ó hEochaidh, Máire Bhríd Ní Cheallaigh, 1946. It appears that snuff is being shared.

Crom Dubh Head in
Churchyard, Cloghane, Co.
Kerry. Crom Dubh might
be regarded variously as a
pagan idol or an image of the
Devil. He is central to the
Sunday closest to the first of
August which is traditionally
celebrated as 'Lughnasa',
'Garland Sunday' or 'Crom
Dubh Sunday'

At harvest time, a three-stranded plait was made from the last standing stalks of corn before being reaped and brought home by the mower to hang above a door as a protective symbol. This practice was known in Armagh as 'cutting the cailleach', cailleach being the Irish word for hag. This photograph was taken in Dromintee, Slieve Gullion, County Armagh in the 1930s.

Landscape with otherworld
associations, looking across
to Cnoc Áine, Teileann,
County Donegal.

May bush, County
Westmeath, 1964.
The May Bush is most
common in Leinster,
although it is also known
in other parts of Ireland.
It is set up outside the
house on May Eve and is
decorated with flowers,
ribbons or pieces of paper.
Whitethorn is the most
popular type of bush.
The May bush signals the
arrival of summer.

Fairy bush, near Glenhull,
County Tyrone.

The Otherworld *Music & Song from Irish Tradition*

The Gold Ring

played on the uilleann pipes by Cormac Cannon

One of the better-known tunes associated with the Otherworld is the 'The Gold Ring', it was said that on hearing fine music, a man followed the sound and came upon the fairies as they were dancing. On observing him, they vanished, leaving behind a gold ring where they had been dancing. He returned it to the fairies who indicated they would grant the man one wish. He requested the best tune they had and was given the tune called 'The Gold Ring'.

Séamus Ennis tells a version of this tale in Irish before playing the tune 'The Gold Ring' on the pipes on *Séamus Ennis: Ceol Scéalta agus Amhráin* (2006).

Cormac Cannon, from Galway, began learning the whistle from Mary Bergin at an early age. He took up the pipes some years later, learning initially from Tommy Keane and later from other prominent players during regular visits to the Willie Clancy summer school held each July in Miltown Malbay, County Clare. He has toured and taught in Ireland, Japan, Africa, the USA and throughout Europe. His recorded output includes *The Cobblestone Sessions* (2002), *Rogha Scoil Samhraidh Willie Clancy* (2008) and a series of albums recorded with his mother, harper Kathleen Loughnane. Cormac has a keen interest in the music of the older pipers and fiddle players, particularly the music of Clare and Kerry, and a preference for the sound of the flat-pitched pipes. On this recording he is playing a set pitched in C# made by Michael Egan around 1850 or so. This set was severely damaged at some time in the past and is the subject of an ongoing restoration project.

The setting of 'The Gold Ring' he plays here is that usually associated with Séamus Ennis, but with an extra part Cormac learned from a recording of Willie Clancy made by Chris Delaney in the 1970s.

'The Piper's Stones', Athgreaney, Hollywood, County Wicklow, 2012. The stones are said to be people petrified for dancing on a holy day.

Halseyrath is the name of a place near Tullycanna, County Wexford. It takes its name from a rath, which is on the edge of a steep, deep glen in the place Aill Suí Ráth.

Local tradition tells us that anyone who ever meddled with this rath was severely punished and chastised for doing so.

About seventy years ago the owner of the farm on which the rath is situated, tilled the rath, after which nearly all his stock died. He even lost most of his family.

When he was selling to the present owners, the last advice he gave them and he leaving was not to ever meddle with this rath.

About a hundred years ago a woman named Whitty went to cut bushes in the rath. There are several bushes and 'sceachs' around it and I suppose she wanted some firewood. She had only just started to break the bushes, or to cut them, when she died.

So much afraid were the people to meddle with this rath that if a child only brought home the smallest piece of stick or firewood, he would be sent back to the rath with it again. The present owners, a Protestant family, told me that at certain times during the year, every year, a dark green circle would appear in the centre of the rath. This was supposed to be the fairies' dancing ring. The ring grew larger every year, till finally it outcircled the rath altogether and it hasn't been seen for the last four or five years.

Told by Mr P. Martin, Tullycanna, County Wexford to Tomás Ó Ciardha, 21.2.1935. (NFC 54: 122-123)

In addition to inhabiting hills, mounds and raths, fairies leave their mark on the landscape in many different ways. Human interference with fairy dwellings almost inevitably brings dangerous repercussions to the mortal sphere. The preceding account underlines how one such negative experience influenced subsequent oral tradition in Tullycanna, County Wexford.

Cormac Cannon

The Fiddler and the Fairy

told by Mickey Doherty

There was an old fiddle player one time lived in Glenfin and he only had the two tunes but he was asked to go to a dance to Letterilly, a townland they call Letterilly. And on his way going, he had the fiddle with him and he didn't care for going, he only had the two tunes. And as he was going along a lonely part of the road there come a wee red-haired man out afore him and the wee man asked him where he was going. He said he was going to a dance in Letterilly and he would far rather not go on account of him only having the two tunes and he knowed there would be a big crowd there and it would be hard to play them the music. The wee man says he to him: 'What kind of a fiddle,' he says, 'have you with you?' So he took the fiddle out from under his coat and he showed the fiddle to the wee man and the wee man examined her. And he run his fingers across the strings three times and he handed the fiddle back to him. 'Well, go on,' says he to this fiddle player, says he, 'go on' he says, 'and don't be cowardly,' he says, 'in going to the dance the night,' he says. There'll be no other fiddle player there,' he says, 'like you.'

So on he went and when he came into the dance house, there was a very big crowd and he took his seat to play for them and when he drew out the fiddle, he drew the bow on her and she was twice as loud and there wasn't a tune of a hundred tunes but he had. They all got up to dance and they said they never heard a fiddler in this world like him. So he played on till the morning and in fact he was able to rise the roof of the house with music. But he was the best fiddle player was supposed to be in this county and he was a good fiddle player all his life and lived to be very old. And when he took death, on his deathbed, the fiddle was hung above him where he was lying and when he departed, the fiddle bursted on the wall. The fiddle bursted on the wall when he departed. He was the name of Herron. He was from a townland they call Garvan Hill.

In this case the magic powers are transmitted to the fiddle rather than directly to the musician. The invocation of special numbers such as three plays an important role in establishing a sense of mystery in many folktales. The gift bestowed on the man and the fiddle is taken away on the death of the musician indicating that powers given by the fairies are often of a temporary nature.

This masterful retelling of a common folk legend is part of the body of material including 'The Jig Learned off the Fairies', recorded on acetate disc from Mickey Doherty, the travelling musician, for the Irish Folklore Commission by Caoimhín Ó Danachair and Seán Ó hEochaidh in a house in the Bluestack Mountains, County Donegal in January 1949.

San am fadó bhí cáil mhór ar cheoltóirí ar fud na hÉireann agus in Albain chomh mhaith. Agus bhí comórtas curtha idir ceoltóirí na hÉireann agus ceoltóirí Alban agus bhí duais mhór ceapaithe do fébrí cén ceoltóir ab fhearr agus a b'fhoghlamta. Ach bhí daoine go leor cruinnithe ins an áit a raibh an comórtas le bheith ar bun an oíche a bhí ceapaithe amach acu leis an gcomórtas a bheith ann. Thosaigh an dá cheoltóir, thosaíodar a seinm i dtús na hoíche agus bhíodar a seinm agus ní mórán a bhí ceapadh cé acub ab fhearr. Ach nuair a bhí deireadh na hoíche teannamh amach ceapadh go mb'fhearr an ceoltóir an tAlbanach. Bhí faitíos ar an Éireannach, ar Hanraí go raibh sé le bheith buailte agus ar maidin, le fáinne an lae, chuaigh sé amach ar an tsráid, agus ní raibh sé mórán achair amuigh nuair a casadh fear dhó agus set píopaí ceoil aige féin faoina ascaill. Agus bheannaigh sé do Hanraí agus dúirt sé:

The Otherworld *Music & Song from Irish Tradition*

Traveller camp,
County Down,
1957.

'Creidim, a Hanraí,' a dúirt sé, 'go bhfuil an ceol ag gabháil crua leat.'

'Tá - ceol ag dul crua liom,' a dúirt Hanraí, 'Tá faitíos orm go bhfuil mé le bheith buailte.'

'Seo dhuit an set píopaí seo atá agamsa,' a dúirt an fear a casadh dhó amuigh, 'agus tabhair domsa na cinn atá agat ar malrait agus buailfidh tú an tAlbanach,' a deir sé, 'nuair a thosós tú a seinm leob seo, tá mise gabháil a thabhairt duit.'

Thóig Hanraí uaidh na píopaí ceoil agus thug sé dhó na cinn a bhí aige féin ar malrait agus tháinig sé isteach insan teach aríst agus ní raibh a fhios ag aon nduine gá raibh istigh nach iad na píopaí a bhí aige i gcaitheamh na hoíche a bhí aige thar éis a thíocht isteach dhó. Agus is én chéad phort a chas sé léis a thíocht isteach 'Máirseáil na Fuiseoige'. Dúirt chuile dhuine go raibh an duais ag gabháil go Hanraí mar chinn sé ar an Albanach 'Máirseáil na Fuiseoige' a chasadh. Agus fuair Hanraí an duais, agus bhí [an] duais an-mhór agus bhí an tAlbanach buailte ar maidin ag Hanraí le 'Máirseáil na Fuiseoige' a chas sé ar na píopaí a fuair sé ón bhfear sidhe a casadh dhó taobh amuigh.

Tá 'chuaigh sé chomh crua leat agus chuaigh an ceol le Hanraí' ina leathdhul sa gceantar seo.

Pádraig Mac Con Iomaire, An Coillín, Carna, Contae na Gaillimhe a d'inis do Liam Mac Coisdeala, 18.11.1935. (CBÉ 158:146)

Long ago, there were famous musicians all over Ireland and in Scotland as well. And a competition was arranged between the Irish musicians and the Scottish musicians. The best, most skilled musician was to be awarded a big prize. A crowd had gathered where the competition was to be held on the appointed night. The two musicians began playing early that night and it was hard to decide who was the better musician. But towards the end of the night it was thought that the musician from Scotland was the better. The Irish musician, Hanraí, was afraid he would lose the competition and at daybreak the following day, he went out and had not gone far when he met a man who had a set of pipes under his elbow. And he greeted Hanraí and said:

'I believe, Hanraí,' he said, 'that you are experiencing difficulty with the music.'

'That is true', said Hanraí. 'I am afraid I will be beaten.'

'Here is my set of pipes,' said the man he met outside, 'and give me your set of pipes in exchange and you will beat the Scot,' he said,' when you begin to play the set I am giving you now.'

Hanraí took the set of pipes from him and gave him his set in exchange and he came into the house again and no one inside was aware of the fact that when he came in he did not have the same set of pipes he had the previous night. And the first tune he played after he came back in was 'The Lark's March'. Everyone said Hanraí deserved the prize because the Scot was unable to play 'The Lark's March'. And Hanraí got the prize and it was a very big prize and Hanraí had beaten the Scot with 'The Lark's March' that he played on the pipes that he got from the fairy man he met outside.

'You found it as difficult as Hanraí found the music' is a saying in this district.

Told by Pádraig Mac Con Iomaire, An Coillín, Carna, County Galway to Liam Mac Coisdeala, 18.11.1935. (NFC 158:146)

Pádraig Mac Con Iomaire's tale explains the origin of a saying in Irish from his native district of Carna, County Galway, which is used when someone finds a particular task to be almost insurmountable. The saying, in translation, says 'You found it as difficult as Hanraí found the music' and is rooted in a version of the well-documented legend of the transfer of music from an otherworld being to a mortal who has been struggling with a limited repertoire of music.

An Mhaighdean Mhara [The Mermaid]

sung by Nóra Dunlop

*Is cosúil gur mheath nó gur thréig tú
an greann,
Tá sneachta go frasach fá bhéal an áith,
Do chúl bhuí daite is do bhéilín séimh,
Seo chugaibh Mary Heeney is í i ndéidh
an Éirne a shnámh.*

*'A mháithrín mhilis,' dúirt Máire Bhán,
Fá bhruach an chladaigh is fá bhéal na trá,
Maighdean mhara mo mháithrín ard,
Seo chugaibh Mary Heeney is í indéidh
an Éirne a shnámh.*

*Tá mise tuirseach agus beidh go lá,
Mo Mháire bhruinneall, mo Phádraig bán,
Ar bharr na dtonnaí is fá bhéal na trá,
Seo chugaibh Mary Heeney is í i ndéidh
an Éirne a shnámh.*

*Is iomaí scéal i mbéaloideas na hÉireann agus
go hidirnáisiúnta faoi dhaoine nó faoi mhuintir
na farraige. Chreidtí go raibh domhan faoi uisce
ann inar mhair neacha cosúil leis an mhaighdean
mhara. Insíodh scéalta agus dúradh amhráin faoin
mhaighdean mhara. Sa seanchas béil, is leagan den
bhfinscéal 'An Fear a Phós an Mhaighdean Mhara'
is cúlra ag an amhrán 'An Mhaighdean Mhara'.
Comhrá atá san amhrán idir an mhaighdean
mhara agus a hiníon Máire.*

Nóra Dunlop

*Phós fear den chine daonna an mhaighdean mhara
agus chuir seisean a clóca i bhfolach agus níor fhéad
sí dul ar ais sa bhfarraige gan a clóca. Bhí muirín
acu. Nuair a tháinig an clóca chun solais, bhí ar an
mhaighdean mhara a dhul ar ais sa bhfarraige arís.
Tá cíoradh déanta ar ghnéithe de thraidisiún na
maighdine mara ag Bo Almqvist (Féach Almqvist
1990, 1999).*

*Tá an nóta seo a leanas sa dialann ag an
mbailitheoir, Mícheál Ó Domhnaill don 22ú
Bealtaine, 1974:*

> *Teach Mhicí Hiúdaí, Rann na Feirste. As
> Machaire Gathlán do Nóra McMonagle.
> Nóra Johnny Bhig (Dunlop) a bhí uirthi sular
> pósadh í. Tá sí tuairim is ar 55 bl. d'aois.*

*Rugadh Nóra Dunlop i dTeach an Bháid i
Machaire Gathlán do John Dunlop agus a bhean,
Madgie. Preisbitéaraigh agus fir farraige ó Albain
agus ó Chontae Aontroma ba ea na Dunlops ach
tógadh glúin John Dunlop mar Chaitlicigh, le
Gaeilge. Bhí Nóra ag teagasc i Scoil an Toir, nuair
a phós sí Paddy Mac Monagail agus shocair siad
i Mín Corrbhaic. Ghlac sí páirt in achan sórt
gníomhaíochtaí fán cheantar.*

*Bhí iomrá ar mhuintir Mhic Mhonagail de bharr
na n-oícheanta airneála a bhíodh acu, oícheanta
go maidin, le hamhránaíocht, scéaltóireacht agus
fidiléireacht. Thiocfadh comharsanaí agus cairde ó
Ghaoth Dobhair agus na Rosa le chéile. Bhí dáimh
mhór idir muintir na gcnoc agus muintir Rann
na Feirste agus bheadh siad ag malairt leaganacha
amhrán, go háirithe. D'fhoghlaim Nóra cuid mhór
amhrán ó sheanfhear as Loch Caol, Paddy Mac
Aoidh. Leaganacha an Toir a deireadh sí, agus
ba ghnáth léi iad seo a chanadh ag na hoícheanta
seo, amhráin mar 'A Chití na gCumann', 'An
Draighneán Donn' agus 'An Mhaighdean Mhara'.
Bhí an ceoltóir agus an bailitheoir Mícheál Ó
Domhnaill i láthair ag ceann de na hoícheanta
airneála seo nuair a chuala sé Nóra ag ceol agus
tháinig sé go luath ina dhiaidh sin le taifeadadh
a dhéanamh. Thaifeadaigh sé cúig cinn déag
d'ámhráin uaithi a raibh cúpla amhrán Béarla
ina measc. Bhuail drochshláinte Páidí agus Nóra i*

1990. Fuair Páidí bás i mí na Bealtaine 1991 agus trí seachtainí ina dhiaidh sin, mí an Mheithimh, lean Nóra é.

The Mermaid

It seems you're in decline and have lost heart,
The snow is plentiful at the mouth of the ford,
Your fair hair and your small gentle mouth,
And here is Mary Heeney and she has crossed the River Erne.

'Dear mother,' said Fair Máire,
At the edge of the shore and the mouth of the sea,
My dear mother is a mermaid,
And here is Mary Heeney and she has crossed the River Erne.

I am weary, and will be until dawn,
My beautiful Máire, my fair Pádraig,
On the crest of the waves and at the mouth of the sea,
And here is Mary Heeney and she has crossed the River Erne.

Irish and international oral traditions contain a number of legends associated with the people of the sea. It was believed by some that an entire world existed under the ocean where beings like the mermaid lived and about whom stories were told and songs were sung. According to tradition, the context of the song 'An Mhaighdean Mhara' ('The Mermaid') stems from the legend 'The Man who Married the Mermaid'. The song takes the form of a conversation between the mermaid and her two children. The legend has it that a mortal man married a mermaid and hid her cloak. She was then unable to return to the sea. The couple had children. When the cloak was discovered, the mermaid felt compelled to abandon her mortal family and return to her original home - the sea. Bo Almqvist has examined some mermaid traditions. (See Almqvist 1990, 1999).

Mícheál Ó Domhnaill wrote the following note in his diary 22nd of May, 1974:

Teach Mhicí Hiúdaí, Rann na Feirste. Nóra McMonagle is from Machaire Gathlán. She was Nóra Johnny Bhig (Dunlop) before she married. She is around 55 years of age.

Nóra Dunlop was born in Machaire Gathlán. Her parents were John Dunlop and his wife, Madgie. The Dunlops were originally Presbyterians from Scotland and County Antrim but John Dunlop's generation were raised as Catholics and were Irish-speakers. Nóra was a teacher in the school in An Tor when she married Paddy Mac Monagail and they settled in Mín Corrbhaic

The Mac Monagail house was renowned for music and entertainment. Nights of songs, stories and fiddle music often continued until the early hours. Neighbours from Gaoth Dobhair and Na Rosa would gather in. The people who lived in the nearby hills and the people of Rann na Feirste were very close to each other and they often exchanged versions of their songs. Nóra learned many songs from Paddy Mac Aoidh, an old man from Loch Caol. She sang versions from An Tor and usually sang them on these occasions. They included songs such as 'A Chití na gCumann', 'An Draighneán Donn' and 'An Mhaighdean Mhara'. Mícheál Ó Domhnaill was present at one of these nights of entertainment and heard Nóra singing. Shortly afterwards he visited her to make some recordings. He recorded fifteen songs from her including some songs in English. In 1990 Páidí and Nóra both suffered ill health. Páidí died in May 1991 and Nóra followed some three weeks later.

Situated about a quarter of a mile south of Bonniconlon is 'Oatlands House'. Long ago there lived a family of the O'Dowd's in that house. One day, as one of them was walking on the shore of Enniscrone, he saw a beautiful lady sitting on a rock combing her hair. The rock was some distance out in the sea, but unaware to the lady, he crouched out as far as the rock and caught hold of her. Then he asked her to go home with him and [said] that he would marry her. The lady consented and after a few days they were married.

The Otherworld Music & Song from Irish Tradition

Then he found out that she was a mermaid and he stole her shroud from her so that she could not return to the sea. He used to hide it in the stack of oats every year. They had three sons and one day they saw their father hiding the shroud in a stack of oats. Shortly afterwards, when he went to town, one of the children told their mother that they saw their father putting a white cloth into a stack of oats. She immediately understood that it was her shroud and set [to] work to find it. When she found it she went towards the sea at Enniscrone bringing with her the three children, but before entering the water she struck them with a wand and turned them into three rocks.

Ever since, the three rocks can be seen on the shore and it is said that anyone the name of O'Dowd that passes by any two of the rocks will die inside a year.

Told by Peter O'Hara (52), Kilgarvin, Bonniconlon, Ballina, County Mayo to Belinda O'Hara in 1938. (NFCS 128: 254-257)

Legends concerning the mermaid are particularly prominent in an island nation and often include motifs where she marries a mortal and bears children before eventually returning to the sea. The breaking of the maternal bond as the mother turns the children to stone and leaves them on dry land while she returns to the sea is particularly dramatic in this telling. The setting here is on a spectacular part of the Sligo coastline and three prominent coastal rocks, known locally as the 'Dowd Stones', are invested with an otherworldly origin.

The Dowd Stones, Scurmore, Enniscrone, County Sligo, 2011.

The Otherworld Music & Song from Irish Tradition

Willie O!

sung by Bernie Lawrence

If this long night was as a dark as dungil,
And no daylight, love and, to appear,
Wouldn't I be guided without one stumble,
Into the arms of you my dear?

Oh, when he came to his true-love's cottage,
He gently kneeled down on a stone.
And through a pane he have whispered slowly:
'Are you my darling that lies alone'?

Oh, she rose up off her soft down pillow,
And snowy, snowy was her milk-white breast:
'Who's that? Who's that at my bed window,
Depriving me of my long night's rest?'

He said: 'I'm your lover, pray don't discover,
So rise up darling, and let me in.
So I'm fatigued after my long journey,
Besides I'm wet, love, into the skin.'

She rose up off her soft down pillow,
And snowy, snowy was her milk white breasts.
They kissed, shook hands and embraced each other,
Until that long night was at an end.

He said: 'Goodbye lover, I can stay no longer,
The burning tempest I have to cross,
Through hills and valleys, I'll rove with pleasure,
This very night, just, it is my last.

This final verse was incomplete in the recorded version:

[They kissed, shook hands and the cock was crowing
She says: 'Willie dear, what have you done?
Where is the blushes you had some years ago?'
'I'm but the ghost of your Willie o!']

The revelation in the final verse normally associated with this song tells us that the departing lover is in fact a ghost. The belief that cock crow signalled a time when ghosts were obliged to return to the spirit realm is reflected in song and story and finds common expression in the vampire legend.

The song is also known as 'Sweet William's Ghost' and 'My Willie' (uí Ógáin/O'Connor 1983). Related versions have been collected in Ireland entitled 'Willie Reilly's Ghost', 'The Bay of Biscay' and 'Here's a Health to My True Lover'. Tom Munnelly included seventeen versions in his index of songs in English in the National Folklore Collection, of which he collected eight versions. He summarised the song in the following manner:

> I will go and see my love though she is far from me. Narrator whispers through her window: 'Are you awake?' 'Who disturbs me at my rest?' 'Your lover, let me in for I am tired and wet after my journey.' He is admitted and they embrace. He tells his love he must go and cross the burning tempest. He bids farewell as the cock crows and tells her he is but the ghost of her Willie-o.

The concept of the return of the dead is well-attested in the song tradition of Ireland. In Irish, an example of a song reflecting this phenomenon is 'Táim Sínte ar do Thuama' ('I am Stretched on Your Grave') which is thematically related to 'Ceaite an Chúil Chraobhaigh' also known as 'Seán Bán'. It takes the form of a conversation between a girl, returned from the dead, and her young man who is still alive. The girl's parents are blamed for not allowing the couple to marry. He says he spends a great deal of time stretched on Ceaite's grave lamenting her death while his parents think that he is asleep.

Overt expressions of intense grief, such as lying prostate on a grave, tearing one's hair and the practice of 'keening' are normally thought of as being the preserve of women. The 'keen' or 'caoineadh' is the crying or wailing performed over the dead at wakes and funerals. The deceased person is often directly addressed in the 'keen'.

Bernie Lawrence was a settled Traveller and Tom made this recording in his home on the Gurteen Road, Boyle, County Roscommon on the 17th of May, 1973. He was then aged sixty-nine. Tom recorded fourteen songs in all from Bernie in what appears to be the only recording session the collector and singer had. Tom wrote in his diary for that day that it took from 11 a.m. until 3 p.m. to persuade Bernie to share some of his songs, when 'he finally gave in and agreed to sing'. Tom said it was worth the trouble and that Bernie had many good songs including a version of 'False Lankum'.

———————

In the olden times the people hadn't any clocks or watches to tell them the time. They used go by the sun during the day and the crow of the cock by night. They never would go in a journey by night till the cock would crow, that would be about half past two or so. They believed that after the cock crowing that the fairies was gone and it was safe for anyone to go out then.

Told by Máire Ní Chinnéide (76), Derrygorman, Keel, Castlemaine, County Kerry to P.J. O'Sullivan, 13.1.1945. She heard it from her mother in 1885. (NFC 744:129)

Máire Ní Chinnéide described for P.J. O'Sullivan some of the significant beliefs and associated practices in relation to the crowing of the cock. The importance of cockcrow can hardly be underestimated at a time when reckoning of hours, days, weather and much else was dependent on inherited oral knowledge.

The Otherworld Music & Song from Irish Tradition

The Otherworld *Music & Song from Irish Tradition*

Travellers, Puck Fair, Killorglin, County Kerry, c.1955. Six of the singers and musicians featured on these recordings are Travellers or settled Travellers.

The Lone Bush

played on the flute by Tara Diamond

A solitary bush or tree, generally whitethorn or hawthorn, is often reputed to be associated with the fairies. Fairies are said to gather, play music and dance around such a tree or bush. Interference by mortals in relation to a lone bush might well incur the wrath of the fairies. Those who cut down a tree for example, risk drawing down their revenge. In recent years, The National Roads Authority rerouted the Ennis by-pass road around a lone bush at Latoon, near Newmarket-on-Fergus in County Clare as the bush was reputed to be especially connected with the fairy host. Peter Clarke, of Bailieborough, County Cavan, aged seventy-four, told the collector P.J. Gaynor in 1942:

There used to be a lone bush in Carroll's yard in Anne St., Bailieboro. One day a bread van driver ...from Kells cut the bush and he was dead in a couple of days.

A man ... gave him a hand at the cutting of the bush and he got a tip of the bush in the eye while they were cutting it and he lost the eye. That would be about fifty years ago. (NFC 832:494-495)

That same year, a blacksmith called Charles Moran also from Bailieborough told the same collector:

I heard of a man called Smith, of Corfad, near Virginia, and he started to cut a lone bush and he got a jag of a thorn in the thumb. He got blood poison in the arm after it, and the arm had to be amputated. The result was that his children got so much afraid that they built stones and clay round the roots of the lone bush to keep it safe. (NFC 832:391-392)

Lone Bush,
Loch an Tóraic,
County Galway,
1939.

The Otherworld *Music & Song from Irish Tradition*

Flute player Tara Diamond comes from Clinch, County Down, but has been living in Dublin since 1987. She learned her early music from her father, Leslie Bingham, who is also a flute player. Tara teaches regularly at the Willie Clancy Summer School, the Frankie Kennedy Winter School, as well as other workshops in Ireland and abroad. Her husband Dermy plays fiddle, as do her son Danny and daughter Helen, who also sings. She recently recorded an album of music with Dermy and Dáithí Sproule.

'The Lone Bush' was composed by fiddle player Ed Reavy (1898 – 1988). Originally from Barnagrove, Maudabawn, County Cavan, where he grew up in a musical family, he emigrated to America in 1912 and settled in Philadelphia, where he spent the rest of his life. He is considered one of the most prolific composers of Irish music during the twentieth century and his tunes, especially his dance music, have been adopted and embraced by Irish traditional musicians all over the world. Many of the titles for Reavy's compositions reflect his memories from his homeland with many bearing place names or features of the countryside associated with his birthplace. 'The Lone Bush' appeared in the first collection of Ed Reavy's tunes *Where the Shannon Rises*, published in 1971 and in the more recent *The Collected Compositions of Ed Reavy*.

Tara Diamond

108

An Aill Eidhneach [The Ivy-Covered Rock]

sung by Ciarán Ó Con Cheanainn

Ag gabháil thríd an Aill Eidhneach go deimhin-mhoch Dé Domhnaigh,
Is ea dhearc mise an mhaighdean chiúin-aigeanta, mhúinte.
Bhí garda ar chaon taobh dhi is bhí 'band' ag seinm cheoil dhi,
Is gur ina timpeall a bhí an t-iontas ag ól fíona agus beorach.

Chrom mé mo cheann síos le fonn a bheith ag éisteacht,
Go bhfeicfinn cén mám é sna cártaí á ndéanamh,
Bhuail suan mé is níorbh é an t-am é is níor chodlaíos ach néal beag,
Is dheamhan pioc a bhí ina háit agam ach an tuláinín sléibhe.

Bheannaigh mé féin dhi de réir mar bhí m'eolas:
'An dócha gur tú Vénus, Brídeach nó Róise?
Ar ndóigh ní tú Créabhrach de chríonchailligh dhóite,
Is gur le méid do chuid draíochta a rinneadh aoileann bhreá óg díot?'

'Go deimhin ní mise aon duine den tsórt sin,
Ach de chlann chlainne Mhaoilís, is na rítí ar fónamh,
Mise Gil-Mhic Ní Mhaolghaoithe is cuimhnigh air i gcónaí,
Is mé banríon na bruíne atá ar mhaoilín Cheann Boirne.

Bhuail slám den cheo draíochta mé is dheamhan pioc ba léir dhom,
Ach ag imeacht cois claí dhom mar bheadh dall ann is mé a sméarthúch,
Shíl mé gurb í an ghrian a d'éirigh is a rinne soilse i mo thimpeall,
Nuair a scal a cuid 'diamonds', an bhreighid bhreá gheal ghléigeal.

Thóig mac Rí Laighean mé le draíocht as a chóiste,
Ach ní bhfuair sé saol coicíse ar ghaidhte mé a phósadh,
B'fhearr liom an mhaighdean ag cur 'silence' ar óigfhir,
Ná a bhfuil d'ór buí is 'diamonds' i gcoillte Chrích Fódla.

The Otherworld *Music & Song from Irish Tradition*

Tugtar le fios san amhrán go bhfaca fear spéirbhean, ón slua sí seans, agus gur thit sé i ngrá léi. Cheap sé gur Bandia nó neach osnádúrtha eile í agus tharla comhrá eatarthu.

Ar ndóigh, is iomaí míniú nó cúlra a thagann i gceist le hamhrán agus mar seo a leanas a thug Mícheál Bheairtle Mac Donncha cúlra an amhráin seo don bhailitheoir Liam Mac Coisdeala ar an 21ú Iúil, 1942:

> *Fear de Pheircíneach a bhí i bpobal Thír an Fhia. Bhí sé féin agus a bhean agus gasúr de mhac a bhí acub ina gcónaí in éineacht. Is bhí gunna sa teach aige. Chuile uair a d'fhághadh an mac aill (seans) ar an ngunna, ghoideadh sé é, nuair a d'fhághadh sé an t-athair imithe ón teach. Is é an t-ainm a bhí ar an mac Mícheál. Ach bhí an t-athair agus an mháthair lá ag gabháil ag trá agus ag gearradh feamainne agus bhí Mícheál a gabháil a fanacht i mbun an tí go dteagaidís. Ach dúirt a athair leis ar a bhfaca sé ariamh gan an gunna a chorraí is dúirt an mháthair leis rud eicint a thabhairt le déanamh dhó a choinneodh ag obair é nó go dteagaidís féin ón trá.*

> *'Tá go maith,' a deir an t-athair. Is thug sé leis tuairim is céad síol coirce i mála agus chraith sé i ngarraí é a bhí spréite ón lá roimhe sin, agus dúirt sé le Mícheál píce a fháil agus a bheith a rucáil sa ngarraí nó go dtagadh sé féin ón trá agus gan corraí as.*

> *'Déanfaidh sin,' a deir Mícheál.*

> *Agus bhailigh an t-athair agus an mháthair leothub agus chuaigh Mícheál ag obair. Agus ní raibh baol ar an trá a bheith thart nuair a bhí an garraí réidh ag Mícheál. Agus chuaigh sé chun an tí agus thug sé leis an gunna. D'imigh leis agus an gunna aige go dtéadh sé ag fiach. Soir leis agus ag gabháil soir thar aill a bhí ann, a dtugann siad an Aill Laighneach [Eidhneach] uirthi, dó chonaic sé faoilleán ina luí ar an aill agus thug sé aghaidh an ghunna uirthi go gcaitheadh sé í. Agus scar an faoilleán a dá sciathán agus dúirt sé ina intinn féin go ligfeadh sé an iarraidh sin léithe. Agus as sin go ceann tamaill thug sé aghaidh an ghunna aríst uirthi agus scar sí na sciatháin aríst agus dúirt sé go ligfeadh sé an darna hiarraidh léi. As sin go ceann tamaill aríst thug sé aghaidh an ghunna uirthi an tríú huair agus rinne sí an cleas céanna.*

'Sílim,' a deir sé ina intinn féin, 'go n-éistfidh mé leat, nach mbeidh dada le déanamh agam leat.'

> *Agus shín sé siar faoi bhun na haille agus thosaigh sé a déanamh amhráin don bhfaoilleán nó go ndearna sé píosa breá d'amhrán dhi. (CBÉ 850:315-316)*

Tá sé ráite gur sa Trá Bhán atá an Aill Eidhneach. (Féach Mac Con Iomaire 34). Bhailigh Máire Áine Ní Dhonnchadha leagan de 'An Aill Eidhneach' samhradh na bliana 1959 i Halla Thír an Fhia ó Bhrídín Ní Chualáin, Leitir Mealláin. Sheinn Liam Mac Con Iomaire an taifeadadh seo ag léacht a thug sé ag Léachtaí Cholm Cille in Ollscoil Mhá Nuad (Mac Con Iomaire) agus bhí Ciarán an-tóigthe leis an amhrán.

B'as Sáile Chuanna, An Spidéal, Ciarán Ó Con Cheanainn (1981 – 2009). Fonnadóir, scoláire agus múinteoir a bhí ann. Bhí sé ar an té ab óige riamh a ghnóthaigh Corn Uí Riada ag comórtas an Oireachtais. Rinne sé céim M.Litt sa Choláiste Ollscoile, Báile Átha Cliath bunaithe ar amhráin a cheantair féin. Tá an leabhar 'Clár Amhrán Mhaigh Cuilinn' (2011) bunaithe ar an saothar sin. Bhí tráchtas dochtúireachta ar siúl aige agus é ag léachtóireacht le Nua-Ghaeilge san ollscoil chéanna. Chuaigh fonnadóireacht Mháire Pheter Uí Dhroighneáin agus Sarah Ghriallais i bhfeidhm go mór ar a chuid amhránaíochta féin.

Ciarán Ó
Con Cheanainn

The Ivy-Covered Rock

**As I went by The Ivy-Covered Rock
early on Sunday,
I spied a quiet, polite young girl,
She was guarded on both sides and
a band was playing music for her,
And around about her many were
drinking wine and beer .**

**I lowered my head in order to listen,
To see what were trumps as the cards
were being dealt,
I fell asleep but it wasn't the right time
and I slept only a little,
And when I woke there was only the
hilly mound.
I greeted her as best I could:
'Are you Venus, Brídeach or Róise?
Or are you Créabhrach the wizened
old woman?
And by the power of your magic
you appear a beautiful young girl?'**

**'Indeed, I am not anyone of that sort,
But one of Maoilís' family,
and of the good kings.
I am Gil-Mhic Ní Mhaolghaoithe and
remember it always,
I am queen of the fort on top of Black Head.**

**Fairy mist overcame me and I could make
nothing out,
As I felt my way along the stone wall as
though blind,
I thought that the sunrise was casting light
around me
When her diamonds shone, fine and bright.**

**The Prince of Leinster in his coach enticed
me by magic,
But he did not survive a fortnight before
being married,
I would rather the young maiden silencing
the young man,
Than all the yellow gold and diamonds
in Ireland.**

The song tells of a man who saw a beautiful woman, possibly from the fairy host, and fell in love with her. He believes she is a goddess or other supernatural being and they converse.

Mícheál Bheairtle Mac Donncha gave the following account of the background to the song to the collector Liam Mac Coisdeala on the 21st of July, 1942:

A man whose surname was Ó Peircín lived in Tír an Fhia. He and his wife and son lived together. And he had a gun in the house. Every time the son got a chance to take the gun, he would steal it, when the father was gone from the house. The son's name was Mícheál. But one day the father and mother were on the beach collecting seaweed and Mícheál was to stay at home to mind the house until their return. And his father told him on no account to touch the gun and the mother said to give him something to do that would occupy him until they would return from the beach.

'Very well,' said the father. And he took around a hundredweight of oat seeds in a bag and spread them around a field that had been laid out the previous day, and he told Mícheál to get a pitchfork and to work in the field until he would return from the field and not to leave it.

'I will do that,' Mícheál.

And the father and mother went off and Mícheál began to work. And the work on the beach was nowhere near to being finished as Mícheál finished the work in the field. And he went to the house and took away the gun. He set off with the gun to go hunting. Off he went and going past a rock they call An Aill Laighneach [Eidhneach], he saw a seagull lying on the rock and he pointed the gun at it to kill it. And the seagull spread its wings and he decided he would let it go this time. And after a while he pointed the gun again and it spread its wings and he said he would let it go the second time. After a while he pointed the gun at it again and it did the same.

'I think,' he said to himself, 'I will leave you alone, that I won't have anything to do with you.'

And he stretched out under the rock and began to make a song for the seagull until he had composed a fine song for it.
(NFC 850:315-316)

An Aill Eidhneach is reputed to be in An Trá Bhán, in Leitir Móir, County Galway. (Mac Con Iomaire 34). The singer, Máire Áine Ní Dhonnchadha collected a version of 'An Aill Eidhneach' in the summer of 1959 in Tír an Fhia Hall, Conamara from Brídín Ní Chualáin, Leitir Mealláin. Liam Mac Con Iomaire, the respected commentator on traditional song, played the recording of Brídín singing the song at a lecture at the National University of Ireland, Maynooth in the series 'Léachtaí Cholm Cille' and Ciarán Ó Con Cheanainn liked the song very much.

Ciarán Ó Con Cheanainn (1981-2009) was from Sáile Chuanna, An Spidéal, County Galway. He was a singer, a scholar and a teacher and was the youngest ever to win the Corn Uí Riada singing competition at the annual cultural festival, An tOireachtas. He completed an MLitt. degree at University College Dublin consisting of an index and catalogue of songs from his native area, which resulted in the publication entitled *Clár Amhrán Mhaigh Cuilinn* (2011). He had begun his doctoral research at University College Dublin and was lecturing in Modern Irish there. He was greatly influenced by the singing of Máire Pheter Uí Dhroighneáin and Sarah Ghriallais.

They say that it was Anna Cliar who put the stones on Bruff Hill. She threw them over from Knockainey Hill, where she used to live and they landed on Bruff Hill. There are big flags of stone, below Knockainey village. Anna Cliar is supposed to have carried these down from one of the quarries on the hill, one by one, and to have set them there.

Told by Thomas Leahy (formerly of Knockainey), Newtown, Bruff, County Limerick to Dáithí Ó hÓgáin, 1971. (NFC 1799:8)

Áine is supposed to be the banshee of Lough Gur, her fairy palace is Cnoc Áine near Kilmallock.

Told by James O'Connell, Oakfront House, Newtownshandon, Charlestown, County Cork to Áine Ní Chróinín, 27.12.1928. (NFC 42:147)

Áine is reputed to have been one of the most important queens of the fairy host. This brief anecdote specifically names the location of her dwelling as a hill which is prominent in the landscape of County Limerick. The narrative also illustrates the change in perception of sovereign goddess and goddess of fertility to queen of the fairy host. The transition of the mythological figure of Áine from goddess to fairy queen reflects changing patterns of folk belief.

Ivy-covered boulder, Camas, County Galway, 1997. Local lore has it that the fairies danced here.

Tam Lin

sung by Áine Furey

'Oh, tell to me, Tam Lin,' she said, 'Why came you here to dwell?'
The Queen of Fairies caught me, when from my horse I fell.

And at the end of seven years, she pays a time to hell,
I so fair and full of flesh and feared it be myself.

For tonight is Halloween and the fairy folk ride,
Those that would let true love win, at Mark's Cross they must by.

So first let pass the horses black and then let pass the brown,
Quickly onto the white steed and pull the rider down.

The first thing that they'll turn me to is into a bear so mild,
So hold me fast and fear me not, I'm the father of your child,

The next thing that they'll turn me to is into a fiery snake,
Hold me fast and fear me not, I'm a man in God's own name.

The next thing that they'll turn me to is into a naked man,
Throw your mantle around my waist and then you have me won.

My woe to you Lady Margaret and an ill death may you die,
You have stolen the noblest lord ever rode in a company.

If I had to know as much last night as I do know the night,
I would have taken his very heart's blood and put in a heart of clay.

Children dressed
for Halloween,
County Wicklow.

The Otherworld *Music & Song from Irish Tradition*

A number of versions of the international ballad 'Tam Lin' were collected in Scotland. It is found in the book *Complaynt of Scotland* which consists of ballads and tales. The book appeared as early as 1549. This song belongs to the 'Border Ballad' tradition – or songs associated with the Scottish/English border.

In Ireland, however, the song appears to have survived in a more fragmented form as found by collectors in the last century. In some instances in Irish tradition 'Tam Lin' appears as a mixture of sung verse and recited prose or chantefable. The singer Eddie Butcher, Magilligan, Count Derry sang a version in this combination in 1975 (Shields 1993 67, 216). Sam Henry collected a substantial version from Alexander Crawford, Leck, Ballymoney, County Antrim but it remains unpublished.

The Journal of the Folksong Society, 1904, contains a version collected by Elizabeth Wheeler from the singing of Ann Carter in Belfast. Ann had learned the song from an old woman in Conamara. The National Folklore Collection contains some accounts indicating that the song may once have been well known, at least in certain localities. In County Donegal, Séamus Ó Gobáin, a farmer from near Ardara, then aged eighty-three, gave a version of the song to the collector Conall C. Ó Beirn on the 2nd of February, 1955. Séamus had heard it from his mother in 1910 when she was sixty years old. He said:

> The old people used to sing what they called 'The Fairy's Song' and I heard an old man in this town singing it, aye, fifty years or more ago. There was a story about the song too but I forget it now.

Séamus then sang the song and concluded with the comment:

> That was what the old people called 'The Fairy Song' and I believe it was about a wane [wee one/child] that was taken and grew up with the wee folk. When the wane was man big it was won back and that is what the song was about. (NFC 1404: 216-218)

A *sidheán* or fairy mound in County Mayo. Note that the bog has been cut away all around for turf supply but the *sidheán* itself is left untouched.

On the 6th of December 1960, Patrick Carre, who farmed in Tullyvoos, Mountcharles, County Donegal, who was then aged 84, gave the version he had heard from his mother to the collector Seán Ó hEochaidh. This was Patrick's account of what he referred to as – 'A Fairy Song':

> The old people used to say that these fairies or wee people took people away with them, especially women, girls and babies. It was a common thing for them to come on Hallow Eve night and take girls away out of face.
>
> They took a girl away one time and there was a song made about her. But some time after, she appeared till a boy that she was great with, and she wanted him to take her back. She told him where they would be riding, and she even told him the colour of the horse that she would be on and for him to try his best to take her back. This was how she put it:
>
> 'Let the black horse by and also let the brown,
> Catch the bay horse by the bridle and pull the rider down.'
>
> The boy did this and when they seen that he did, the first thing they done was to turn her into a snake. She says then:
>
> 'Hold me hard and fear me not, I'm one of God's own make.'
>
> So he held on to her till day broke and once day broke they were finished with her and she was free. They weren't at all pleased when they couldn't take her, and this was how they put it:
>
> 'If we had known this one hour before day,
> We would have cut out this manly heart and put in a heart of clay.'
>
> I often heard my mother at this song when I was small, but I only remember a couple of lines of it now. (NFC 1578:163-164)

The collector Tom Munnelly included numerous references to 'Tam Lin' in his essay on the supernatural in song entitled, 'They're there all the same!' In 1963, Leo Corduff and Seán Ó hEochaidh recorded some of Patrick's lore on tape, which included much fairy material.

Áine Furey lives and works in Dublin. Áine has performed worldwide with her older brother Martin in their band 'Bohinta' ('Badhbh Chaointe') for which Martin writes most of the material they perform. She has studied Irish Folklore and is a member of the well-known Furey family. She got the words of the song in the National Folklore Collection and the air from her father and uncle. The song was popularised during the folk revival of the 1960s and has been widely recorded.

On Hallow eve night you wouldn't be let throw out any water, afraid you would throw it on some spirit that might be outside.

Told by Charles King (60) Murmod, Virginia, County Cavan to P.J. Gaynor, 22.12.1941. (NFC 815:16)

The inter-seasonal festival of Oíche Shamhna or Halloween is a time when the utmost caution is prescribed in venturing out as the spirit world is at its most active at this time between two seasons. It has been recorded that many people in Ireland would shout a warning to the fairies before emptying water vessels outside their house. Halloween, or the eve of the feast of All Souls, is still marked with bonfires, disguise and divination.

Cailín Deas Crúite na mBó
[The Pretty Girl Milking the Cows]

sung by Patrick de Búrca

Amhrán beannaithe é seo ach is amhrán é a bhfuil blas osnádúrtha ag roinnt leis freisin. Moltar go láidir do dhaoine saol a chaitheamh de réir dhlíthe na heaglaise Caitlicí agus luaitear teideal an amhráin sa líne dheireanach den chéad cheathrú 'cailín deas chrúite na mbó'. Tugann an líne amhráin eile chun cuimhne a bhfuil an teideal céanna seo orthu. Meabhraíonn seo freisin an finscéal a insítear faoin amhrán, amhrán a bhfuil leagan gáirsiúil de ar fáil chomh maith. Sagart a bhí ar ghlaoch ola uair amháin agus chuala sé guth cailín, nó in amanna cú dubh, ag fonnadóireacht. Bhí an ceol chomh hálainn gur stop sé le cluais a thabhairt don cheol. Cuireadh moill ar an sagart agus fuair an fear tinn bás sular shroich an sagart é leis an ola dheireanach a chur air. Ba é an Diabhal, is cosúil, ba chúis leis an gceol a chur i mbealach an tsagairt agus d'éirigh leis an Diabhal anam an fhir a thabhairt leis dá réir sin. Cuirtear ábhar gáirsiúil i láthair i gcuid de na leaganacha den amhrán agus cailín saolta a deir an t-amhrán. Le cúiteamh a dhéanamh sa bpeaca a bhí déanta nuair a dúirt sí amhrán chomh gránna sin, bhí i gceist náire a chur ar an gcailín agus go ndéarfadh sí an t-amhrán gáirsiúil ón altóir ag Aifreann an Domhnaigh ach ba é an t-amhrán cráifeach a dúirt sí, faoi mar a dúirt Patrick de Búrca é agus é lán le híomhánna deabhóideacha.

Agus éirígí a pheacaigh agus músclaí,
Agus cuimhnigí ar Aon-Mhac na hóighe.
Is ná smaoinigí ar pheaca na drúise,
Ná ar bhealach gach cúilínín óig.
Ach guígí na haingle dhár gcumhdach,
Is ar Mhaighdean bhreá chumhachtach
na nglór,
Is nach fearr dhíobh í mar charaid lá
an chuntais,
Ná cailín deas chrúite na mbó.

Agus an trua libhse lucht drainnimh
agus drúise,
Lucht meisce, lucht drúise agus póit,
Bhíonns ag éirí ar maidin Dé Domhnaigh,
Agus ag caitheamh mímhúin ag tí an óil.
Ná faillígí an tAifreann ar aon chor,
Mar níl sólás fán saol seo níos fearr,
Ach guígí míle is céad buíochas,
Leis an tAon-Mhac a d'fhulaing a gcáis.

Agus tiocfaidh an tArd-Phrionsa gan amhras,
Is beidh an chlann bhocht ag ins[eacht],
ó, na ndeor,
Is níl onóir dár cumadh ná dá gcumtar,
Nach mbeidh againn ansiúd os a chomhair.
Agus tréigfidh an fharraige an-bhrúidiúil,
Agus silfidh gach neoin-charraig bréan,
Is nuair a shéidfeas an t-aingeal an trumpa,
Beidh gach anam ina dhlúthcholainn féin.

Agus tiocfaidh Mac Muire dár bhféachaint,
Is beidh an chlann bhocht uilig os a comhair,
Is teannóm liomsa is céad fáilte,
Don chathair a gheall Mac Dé dhúinn,
A Mhaighdean bhreá chumhachtach
atá láidir,
Nach tú barr agus áilleacht gach ciall,
Nach tú onóir agus urlár na práinne,
Agus molaigí go hard ainm Chríost.

Bhí ainm in airde ar Patrick (nó Pat) Phádraig Liam), An Aird Mhóir, Carna, Contae na Gaillimhe, mar fhonnadóir agus rinne sé amhráin agus véarsaíocht chomh maith. Nuair a bhí Séamus Mac Aonghusa ina bhailitheoir ceoil agus amhrán ag Coimisiún Béaloideasa Éireann (1942-1947), thóg sé dhá amhrán ó Patrick. Maidir le ceann de na hamhráin sin 'Bainis Jimí Joe', scríobh Mac Aonghusa: 'ba rí-dheas liom é mar amhrán agus bhí Pádraig de Búrca in ann é chur uaidh gan lucht'. Thug sé leis cuid mhór dá chuid amhrán ó Vail Bheairtle agus ó Mhícheál Bheairtle Ó Donncha. Thug sé cuid mhór amhrán do Chnuasach Bhéaloideas Éireann. Ba nia é leis an scéalaí mór le rá, Éamon de Búrca. Fuair Patrick bás sa mbliain 1996.

The Pretty Girl Milking the Cows

This is a religious song but one with supernatural overtones. The pious exhortation urged on the listener is set in relief by the last line of the first verse which directly refers to the 'Pretty Girl Milking the Cows'. This reference points to other songs bearing this title and to the legend that commonly surrounds this sometimes bawdy song. A priest on a sick call to the bed of a dying man encounters either a young girl or, in some versions, a black hound and becomes entranced by their singing. This delay causes the mortally ill man to die before the priest can administer the last rites and as a result, the Devil claims another soul. In some versions of this tale the song that detains the priest has a pronounced sexual content and is sung by a mortal girl. To publicly shame the girl the priest insists she must sing the same song from the altar at Sunday Mass but in fact, the words that emerge carry the powerful religious imagery found in the version sung here by Patrick de Búrca.

Rise up sinners and awake,
And think of the only Son of the Virgin,
Do not consider the sin of adultery,
Or the way of every young girl.
But pray to the angels, who protect us,
And the fine Virgin Mary of power and glory,
Is she not a better friend on judgement day
Than the pretty girl milking the cows?

Do you pity sinners and adulterers
Drunkards, adulterers and drinkers,
Who get up every Sunday morning,
And frequent the alehouses?
Don't ever neglect Mass,
There is no greater solace in this life.
But give a hundred thousand thanks,
To the only Son who suffered on our behalf.

And the High Prince will certainly come
And the poor children will shed tears,
And every honour that exists,
Will be there before us.
And the powerful sea will recede,
And every rough rock will ooze,
And when the angel sounds the trumpet,
Every soul will be in its own body.

Patrick de Búrca

The Otherworld Music & Song from Irish Tradition

The Otherworld *Music & Song from Irish Tradition*

**And the Son of Mary will come to see us,
And all the wretched people will be
before her,
Come with me and a hundred welcomes,
To the city the Son promised us.
Oh Virgin most powerful,
Are you not the most beautiful possible,
Are you not our support and our rock in
time of need?
And you should greatly praise the name
of Christ.**

Patrick (Patrick Phádraig Liam), Aill na Brón, Carna, County Galway, was a well-known and highly regarded singer. He also composed songs and verse. During his time as collector with the Irish Folklore Commission (1942-1947), Séamus Ennis collected two songs from Patrick. He was a nephew of the famed storyteller Éamon de Búrca. Patrick died in 1996 in his early seventies. He had a large repertoire of songs, most of which he sang in a definite, rhythmic style. Many of them were composed locally and are not often heard outside the Conamara Gaeltacht. Patrick learned many of his songs from two local poets, brothers Vail Bheairtle and Mícheál Bheairtle Ó Donncha.

..agus is gearr go dtaga cogadh agus trioblóid agus an fear a dtugann siad antichrist *air tá sé le thíocht go gairid agus déanfaidh sé sin a shiúil le daoine an domhain ach beagán atá ceaptha ag Dia do dhaoine naofa a bheidheas in ann siúl amach thrí chnoc agus dá mbeadh an cnoc sin trí lasadh le tine dhearg – go ngabhfaidís amach thríd gan iad a dhó. Agus níl éinne le fanacht beo léis* anti-christ *– is gearr uait anois é – ach daoine a shiúlfadh amach thrí chnoc a bheadh trí lasadh le tine agus nach ndóighfí é. Agus beidh dhá mhíle eile de shaol eile ann ina dhiaidh seo, i ndiaidh an dá mhíle seo agus aon mhíle amháin ina dhiaidh sin agus lá an bhreithiúnais ansin.*

Seán Mac Conraoi (84), Cloch na Rón, Contae na Gaillimhe a d'inis do Bhrian Mac Lochlainn, 13.9.1936. (CBÉ 237:127-128)

..and war and trouble will come and the man they call antichrist is due to come shortly and he will walk among the people of the earth but only a few holy people that God has chosen will be able to walk out through the hill and if that hill were ablaze with fire – they will go through it without being burned. And no one will remain alive after the antichrist – his time is close now – except for anyone who could walk out through a blazing hill and would not be burned. But there will be two thousand years of life after that. After that two thousand and one thousand after that again, and then the day of judgement.

Told by Seán Mac Conraoi (84), Cloch na Rón, County Galway to Brian Mac Lochlainn, 13.9.1936. (NFC 237:127-128)

In Irish folk eschatology or belief associated with the end of the world, the image of an antichrist heralding the beginning of the end of time occurs in song and in narrative. The above piece is an example of this belief as told by Seán Mac Conraoi. Along with dramatic apocalyptic imagery, the concept of a 'chosen' people is highlighted.

A Fairy Dance

played on the fiddle by Máire O' Keeffe

Rathlin, off the coast of County Antrim, is the most northerly of Ireland's islands. The tune, 'A Fairy Dance', was collected on Rathlin in 1937 from one of the island's residents, Mrs Katie Glass (1859–1954). The collector was Nils Holmer from Kalmar in Sweden who visited Rathlin in the summer months of 1937, and again in October 1938, to document the spoken Irish of Rathlin. At the time, Mrs Glass, who was then seventy-eight, lived above Mill Bay on Rathlin where she and her parents had been born and raised. Holmer wrote:

> Her grandfather married a Kintyre woman, a Miss Cameron from Tarbert, and it is from her Mrs Glass has got most of her songs and short stories. They are consequently not Irish, though the language is coloured by the Rathlin dialect. (NFC 593:229)

She was listed by Holmer as one of nineteen Irish speakers on the island at the time. Irish has not survived as an everyday language on the island.

> Mrs Glass had an uncle reputed to be a famous piper and, according to her, he was the source of 'A Fairy Dance' having, as he claimed, heard it among the hills. In an account related to Nils Holmer, Mrs Glass described how she and her friend, when passing a fairy fort late at night, would sing the tune. They hoped that the music would coax the fairies to come out and dance so that the two friends might catch a glimpse of them. (NFC 657: 384)

Mrs Katie Glass

When anything was spilled or dropped from the table they used to say 'Och, leig dó. Tá iad feidhmiúil atá feitheamh air', [Leave it. Those that are waiting for it have need of it.] meaning that 'na daoine cóir' or the fairies, expected to get such things.

Told by Mrs Katie Glass to Nils Holmer in 1937. (NFC 593:229)

The voice came to a woman, telling her and her husband to go and dig at a certain place, and she would get silver, but she must not take a stranger with her. She did not heed the voice, but after a while it was heard again. The third time the woman went to the appointed place, bringing her husband and a neighbour with her. They digged, and found nothing. The voice then told her: 'Thú (pron. 'ú') dhona, dhona! Thug thú leat fine coimhthíoch! [You are very bad.] You brought the stranger with you

Told by Mrs Katie Glass to Nils Holmer in 1937. (NFC 593:229)

A boy in Rathlin went out late at night to the shore, and found a whistle on the 'cladach' [shore]. He took it up, and put it to his mouth and blew it. At this time, some people rose up to their elbows. The boy got frightened, and threw away the whistle, and made off. The (dead) men called out after him. 'B'fhearr mar a bhá sinn, ach mar a tá sinn!' [better as we were, than as we are] If he had blown the whistle another time they would have risen to their feet.

Told by Mrs Katie Glass to Nils Holmer in 1937. (NFC 593: 230)

In addition to the tune and lore relating to 'A Fairy Dance', Mrs Katie Glass also contributed the three preceding items associated with otherworld belief.

The tune is played here by Tralee born fiddle player, Máire O'Keeffe. Máire now lives in Kinvara, County Galway where she is a school teacher. Her Ph.D. thesis *Journey into Tradition: A Social History of the Irish Button Accordion*, was completed at the University of Limerick. Máire's fiddle playing can be heard on the cd *Cóisir:*

'A Fairy Dance' – account and transcription by Nils Holmer.

House Party, which was recorded in Cape Breton and she can also be heard on a number of other recordings including *Re-Joyce: Tunes and Songs from the Joyce Collection*. In 2006, Máire initiated the *Joseph Browne Spring School of Traditional Music* in memory of Joseph Browne who was a fiddle pupil of hers and the school takes place annually during the month of February.

Nils Holmer

The Otherworld *Music & Song from Irish Tradition*

Port na Sióg [The Tune of the Fairies]

lilted by Peait Sheáin Ó Conaola

The Otherworld *Music & Song from Irish Tradition*

Mar seo leanas a d'inis Peait an scéal a bhaineann leis an bport:

Casfaidh mé an port seo dhuitse anois, a Chiaráin. Bhíodh sé ag seanfhear sa mbaile agus is minic a d'airínn a rá gur 'Port na Sióg' a thugaidís air.

Beirt fhir bhí siad ag faire bó a bhí le lao aon uair amháin agus roimh an maidneachán lae thosaigh fear acu a casadh port agus d'éirigh fir bheaga bhídeacha amach ón aill agus thosaigh siad a damhsa ach choinnigh sé air a casadh an phort nó gur bhlaoigh an coileach agus ansin nuair a bhlaoigh, tháinig fear acu, duine acu go dtí é. 'Má stopfá roimh ghairm na gcoileach,' a deir sé, 'bhí tú réidh. Mharódh muid thú nó, bhí siad, dhéanfaidís rud éicint leis. Ach siod é an port anois.

Dúirt Peait le Ciarán gur thóig sé an port ó fhear de Mhaolánach 'Micilín Sara' a bhí thart sa mbaile.

Bhí go leor seanphoirt ag Micilín agus ba mhinic a bhíodh Peait thuas sa teach aige. Bhí an-phort ag máthair Pheait freisin. B'uncail do Pheait Martin Mháirtín Neile agus bhí an-phort aige agus b'an-damhsóir a bhí ann. B'annamh bosca ceoil ná meileoidean ag bainiseachaí ach port béil den chuid ba mhó a bhíodh ann.

Is leagan é 'Port na Sióg' den ríl 'The Shaskeen Reel' atá coitianta i measc ceoltóirí. Is iomaí taifeadadh den ríl seo ann. Is deacair a chinntiú cén chaoi ar baisteadh an teideal 'Port na Siógaí' uirthi. Tharlódh gur ainm áitiúil ar an ríl é. Rinne Michael Coleman é a thaifeadadh ar cheirnín 78 agus rinne banna céilí Bhaile na Cille ó oirthear na Gaillimhe é a thaifeadadh chomh maith.

Iascaire a bhí in Peait i mBaile na Creige, Árainn. Chaith sé tamall ag obair i nGaillimh. Sheinneadh sé an cairdín agus bhíodh damhsaí sa teach, faoi mar a bhí i mórán chuile theach in Inis Mór san

Hawthorn bushes in the field of James Murphy (Jemmy Ned). Michael J. Murphy heard Jemmy say of these bushes: 'The hottest day in the summer and it would starve [freeze] you in there in them bushes'.

am. Ní raibh sé pósta. D'imigh an chuid is mó dá mhuintir go Boston Mheiriceá. Fuair Peait bás deireadh na 1960idí.

Thosaigh Ciarán Bairéad ag obair do Choimisiún Béaloideasa Éireann i 1951. Bhí sé fostaithe mar chláraitheoir ar feadh tréimhse go dtí gur ceapadh ina bhailitheoir lánaimseartha é. Ina dhiaidh sin, bhí sé ag obair i gContae na Gaillimhe, i Maigh Eo agus i gContae an Chláir. Choinnigh sé air ag obair mar bhailitheoir lánaimseartha go dtí gur cailleadh é i 1976.

The Tune of the Fairies

Peait's introduction to the tune, as he told it to the collector Ciarán Bairéad, translates:

I'll lilt this tune for you now, Ciarán. An old man around here had it and I often heard it said that they called it 'Port na Sióg' (The Tune of the Fairies). Two men were seeing to a cow in calf once and before daybreak one of them began to lilt a tune and a crowd of tiny little men came out from the cliff and began to dance. He kept up the tune until the cock crew and when it did, one of the men came to him: 'Only that you kept it up, if you had stopped before the cock crew,' he said, 'you were finished. We would have killed you or else the others would have done something to you. But this is the tune now.'

Peait told Ciarán that he got the tune from a local man called 'Micilín Sara' who was of the Ó Maoláin family. Micilín had a lot of old tunes and Peait spent a great deal of time in his house. Peait's mother also had a wealth of tunes. An uncle of Peait's, Martin Mháirtín Neile had many tunes and was a talented dancer. Peait recalled that lilting was the most frequent type of music heard at weddings, as melodeons and accordions were scarce in late nineteenth-century Conamara.

The common name for this is 'The Shaskeen Reel.' A widely recorded and popular tune, it is difficult to say how it gained the title, 'Port na Sióg.' It may simply be a local name. It was recorded, for example on 78s by Michael Coleman of Sligo and the Ballinakill Céilí Band from east Galway.

Peait was a fisherman and lived in Baile na Creige, Inis Mór, Aran Islands. He spent some time working in Galway. He played the accordion at the many house dances which were popular on

Ciarán Bairéad

The Otherworld *Music & Song from Irish Tradition*

The Otherworld *Music & Song from Irish Tradition*

Inis Mór. Peait was unmarried. On emigrating many Conamara people settled in Boston, MA and most of Peait's family members made the same journey leaving little memory of him now on the island. Peait died in the late 1960s.

Ciarán Bairéad started work with the Irish Folklore Commission in 1951. He was employed as a cataloguer for a short period until his appointment as a full-time collector. Subsequently, he worked in counties Galway, Mayo and Clare. He continued to work as full-time collector until his death in 1976.

Bhí fidileoir ina chónaí thiar anseo ar an Chaiseal; fuair sé bás bordaithe trí scór bliain ó shin, agus deireadh an seanbhunadh i gcónaí nach raibh an dá fhidileoir in Éirinn ab fhearr nó é féin agus a dhearthair. Bhí a dhearthair ins na police ins an am thiar ins an áit a dtugann siad Dundalk air. Shiúladh sé féin bunús na hÉireanna. Chaitheadh sé an geimhreadh siar Connachta. Is é an obair a bhí aige damhsaí pínne aige ag tógáil airgid agus ag saothrú páighe ag daoiní eile a seinm díofa, ag bainseacha, baistíocha agus an uile shórt eile den chineál. Is é an t-ainm bheireadh siad air John Mhósaí agus Muiris Mhósaí ar a dhearthair. Ba Mhac Fhionnlaoich iad.

Bhí sé oíche amháin thoir an áit a dtugann siad Mín na Croise air ag seinm ag damhsa go dtí go raibh sé déanach go maith san oíche ag teacht abhaile dó. Bhí sé nó seacht de mhílte aige le siúl abhaile de bhealach uaigneach a mbíodh iomrá go mbíodh mórán taibhsí air agus áiteacha uasal. Ach bhí sé ag teacht anuas ag creig a dtugann siad Creig Bhiodóige uirthi atá cumhdaithe le heidheann agus mórán scealpaíní inti agus ar mhullach na screige seo tá ballóg ann a dtugann siad ballóg Bhiodóige uirthi. Bhuail an fhidileoracht astoigh sa chreig, agus ní raibh aon nduine leis ach é féin agus sheas sé ar an bhealach mhór, agus thug sé éisteacht go dtí go raibh an tiúin seinnte. Tharraing sé ar an bhaile ansin agus nuair a shuigh sé ag an teinidh, i ndiaidh a dhul abhaile, thug sé leis an fhideal agus bhi an tiúin piocaithe suas aige. Sheinn sé an tiúin ar

an fhideal agus is é an t-ainm a bheir siad i nGleann uirthi go fóill 'A Fairy Reel' agus sin an dóigh a dtáinig sí.

Seán Mac Giolla Easpaig (56), Ceann na Coilleadh, Gleann Cholm Cille, Contae Dhún na nGall a thug do Sheán Ó hEochaidh, 22.4.1936. Bhí sé cloiste ag Seán Mac Giolla Easpaig ag an tseanbhunadh thart ar tríocha bliain roimhe sin agus bhíodarsan aosta an uair sin. (CBÉ 179: 552-554)

There was once a fiddle player who lived here in An Caiseal; he died around sixty years ago and the old people always said there were no two better fiddle players in Ireland than he and his brother. His brother was in the police at the time; over in a place they call Dundalk. He used to travel all around Ireland. He would spend the winter in Connachta. His work was playing at penny dances and collecting money and earning his pay by playing music for people at weddings, christenings and all kinds of similar occasions. They called him John Mhósaí and his brother Muiris Mhósaí. Their surname was Mac Fhionnlaoich.

One night, he was in a place they call Mín na Croise playing at a dance until it was quite late in the night after which he was making his way home. He had to walk six or seven miles on a lonely road that was reported to have ghosts and fairy haunts along the way. When he was coming by a rock they call Creig Bhiodóige that is covered with ivy and has numerous crevices in it and on top of this there is a ruin they call Biodóg's ruin. The fiddle music sounded in the rock and he was alone and he stood out on the road, and listened until the tune had been played. He went on home then and when he sat by the fire, after arriving home, he took the fiddle and he had picked up the tune. He played the tune on the fiddle and in Gleann the tune is still called 'A Fairy Reel' and that is how it came there.

Told by Seán Mac Giolla Easpaig (56) Ceann na Coilleadh, Gleann Cholm Cille, County Donegal to Seán Ó hEochaidh, 22.4.1936. Seán Mac Giolla Easpaig had heard it from older people around thirty years previously and they were quite old at the time. (NFC 179: 552-554)

John and Muiris Mhósaí Mac Fhionnlaoich were sons of the blacksmith Moses Mac Fhionnlaich whose forge was at Loch Inse just off the road between Carrick and Gleann Cholm Cille in south-west Donegal. John Mhósaí was born in the mid-nineteenth century and was held in very high regard by generations of fiddle players, among them the Doherty family, who considered him to be one of the best.

The mysterious transfer of a particular tune to a mortal musician is conveyed in Seán Mac Giolla Easpaig's story, which may be traced in this district to the late nineteenth century and may well be considerably older. The legend gives validation within oral tradition to the origin of the tune name 'The Fairy Reel'.

The Fairy Fort

told by Paddy Hedderman

My father used to tell a story one time about the little men appearing to him and telling him: 'You go back there fairly often. The fairies used hurl out on the hill out in the field. They'll be out there hurling some night and they'll ask you to come in hurling with them and don't take a hurley from any one of them. Go home.'

Fairies are said to behave in the manner of humans in most respects. Their food, amusements and life style appear to form a parallel world to that of mortals. They are said to play hurling and football - individually and also in groups. Hurling is the national sport of Ireland and is a team game played with specially designed wooden sticks or hurleys. Hurling and football matches were a common occurrence in the fairy world.

Paddy Hedderman spoke of the fairy raths or liosanna in Bruree and of their association with the Otherworld. Two in particular, known locally as 'Raheens', are circular forts. When Paddy was young it was believed you should not pass these after midnight. His father told him stories of the fairies coming to play hurling. Stories of fairy hurling were also told about a place called Knockfierna, Ballingarry Hill not far from the Hedderman home. Paddy said that the stories came down through history and that it was not possible to trace their origin. He was of the opinion that the generation who believed such stories had passed on.

The recording was made on the 12th of May, 1986 in Paddy Hedderman's house at Mount Eagle, Bruree, County Limerick. Paddy was

Corn stooks of four sheaves in a field with fairy rath or fort in the background, Loughinisland, County Down, 1962.

born in the village of Bruree on the 1st of January 1917, in a house beside St Munchin's holy well; thus, his middle name was 'Munchin'. In the early 1920s, a time of significant political upheaval, he moved to live with an uncle and aunt at Mount Eagle and later inherited their house. He worked for forty-seven years with Córas Iompair Éireann, the Irish national bus and rail company, and was extremely involved in local history, Irish and folklore throughout his life. He died in 1992.

'Twas often my grandfather saw the good people hurling by night down in the inches near the Lios. They could hear them pucking the ball and the 'huzzah' when a goal was scored.

Told by Pádraig Mac Cárthaigh, Knockaneigh, Carbury West, County Cork to Diarmuid Ó hUallaigh, 6.12.1937. (NFC 437:389)

The 'good people' played hurling late at night close to their place of habitation. The game of hurling involves skill, speed and dexterity. It would be impossible for mere mortals to play in darkness. The sights and sounds experienced by the narrator's grandfather above will be familiar to followers of hurling today.

Paddy Hedderman

The Otherworld Music & Song from Irish Tradition

Iomáin Áth na gCasán
[The Annagassan Hurling Match]

sung by Máire Ní Choilm

Ag gabháil go hÁth na gCasán domh, is é casadh orm an slua san oíche,
Is ansin a bhí an iomáin ba deise, a raibh in aird den tsaol.
Bhí na mílte de lucht breacáin ann is lucht boinéadaí ó Aberdeen,
Gur chuir siad mé as mo latitiúd is nárbh fheasa domhsa an lá ón oíche.

A ndul chun an mhuilinn gaoithe domh, bhí fiche fear i mo dhiaidh le ruaim,
Bhí an balla leo go faobhrach is iad scaoilt óna mbásta suas.
Bhuail mise an boc sin tríothu go croíúil is go láidir luath,
Ach is mise a tharla in íochtar ag an chaoilteachán de ghasúr rua.

D'éirigh mé go feargach chun argain a dhéanamh leo,
Ach do buaileadh fúmsa an barrchois agus tiontaíodh mé ar thaobh an róid.
Thug mé an dara hionsaí le cinseal ar an té ba mhó,
Is nach mise bhí sa chontúirt dá n-inseoinn mo scéal ar ndóigh.

Tógadh suas an balla is níorbh fhoráil nó bheadh ann coirp,
Agus bhí muidne uile ag iomrascáil go raibh muid ag bun an chnoic.
Ach murab é an lán mara a chuir bascadh ar an tréanfhear dheas,
Ba bhua a bheadh orm nó chaillfí mé le doirn ina measc.

Tháinig duine uasal barrúil sásta, a chuir bascadh orthu ón taobh ó dheas,
'Stadaigh de bhur ráfla, is ná spárálaigí cos nó cleas.'
Rug buachaillí Bhaile Shláine greim lámha ar na breacáin bhras.
Is ansin a bhí an spairn ar Thrá na bhFaoileán Deas.

Is ansin a bhí an scaifte maighdean ba seasaí a bhí le fáil,
Bhí gríosadh ar lasadh ina n-éadain is a mbéilíní deasa tana tláth,
A gcaoinchoim cailce gléigeala ag éirí mar eala ón tsnámh,
Is iad uilig go haerach i bpléisiúr le ceannaí an tsnáith.

Bhíodh amhráin i gcuimhne ar chluichí móra iomána nó peile coitianta. Is cluiche iomána de chuid na sí atá i gceist san amhrán seo a raibh an file páirteach ann de bharr a bheith amuigh mall san oíche. Lonnaítear an cluiche in Áth na gCasán i gContae Lú. Ba bhreá leis an lucht sí an duine saolta a bheith ina measc – agus ar ndóigh faoi chumhacht acu – agus iad ag spraoi faoi sholas na gealaí. In amanna, chrochadh na sióga daoine ón saol seo leo le píosa oibre faoi leith a dhéanamh, le bheith ar fhoireann do chluiche, nó díreach lena thabhairt ar eachtra scanrúil ar dhroim capaill. Nuair a d'fhágadh na sióga an duine saolta ar ais ar an ngnáthshaol arís, ba mhinic buachalán buí i ngreim ina láimh aige in áit an chapaill sí a bhí á iompar. I Rann na Feirste ba ghnách cur síos ar réalt reatha, ar a dtugtaí caor thine sa ghnáthchaint, mar liathróid i gcluiche iomána idir sióga Chonnacht agus Uladh.

Thosaigh Máire ag cur suime sna hamhráin Ghaeilge nuair a bhí Nellie Eoghain John Shéimí, Nelllie Nic Giolla Bhríde, mar mhúinteoir aici. Bhí an-tionchar ag Áine bean Uí Ghallchóir, Annie John ar a cuid amhránaíochta freisin. Chaith Máire tamall ina múinteoir scoile agus tá sí ag obair faoi láthair i Roinn na Gaeilge i gColáiste Phádraig i nDroim Conrach. Bíonn sí ag freastal ar go leor féilte agus tugann ceardlanna amhránaíochta in áiteacha éagsúla in Éirinn agus thar lear.

Máire Ní Choilm

The Annagassan Hurling Match

As I was going to Annagassan,
I met the host at night,
The best hurling took place that was
ever played,
There were thousands dressed in plaid
and bonnets from Aberdeen,
They put me sideways,
and I couldn't tell day from night.

As I was going to the mill twenty angry men
followed me,
Their blood was up and they were stripped
for action,
I hit that fellow who was among them,
with vigour, strength and speed,
But I came off worse because of the thin
redhaired lad.

I arose angrily to destroy them,
But I was kicked and thrown on
the side of the road,
I made a second attack to overcome
the biggest of them,
But if the truth is told, I was in danger.

The wall was knocked and I was sure there
would be death.
And we were all wrestling until we reached
the bottom of the hill,
And if not for the full tide that vanquished
the fine, strong man
I would have been beaten and felled in
a hail of fists.

A stranger of noble bearing came from
the south warning them,
'Stop your chatter and use might and main.'
The boys from the town of Slane got hold
of the plaid kilts,
And then there was fighting on the pleasant
Gull's Strand.

It was there was found a steadfast group
of girls,
With rosy cheeks and lovely little mouths.
Their slender waists as enticing as the
swan rising from the water,
And they were all happy in pleasant
company with the yarn merchant.

The Otherworld *Music & Song from Irish Tradition*

Songs to commemorate famous hurling or football matches were a feature of folk poetry. This song, situates the events in Annagassan, County Louth and concerns a fairy hurling match in which the poet became involved through his rambling late at night. Nothing pleased the fairies more than to have a mortal in their midst – and of course in their power – during their moonlight revels. Humans could often be carried off at night by fairies, sometimes taken to perform a specific task, other times to help make up a team for a sporting event or simply spirited away on horseback on a frightening adventure. On returning to the mortal world the human taken by the fairies finds the only trace of the otherwordly horse they had ridden is replaced by a 'buachalán buí' or yellow ragwort grasped still in their hand. In Rann na Feirste, County Donegal, a shooting star or thunderbolt was identified as the ball in a hurling match between the Connacht and Ulster fairies.

Máire Ní Choilm's interest in traditional song was sparked by her teacher Nellie Eoghain John Shéimí, Nellie Nic Giolla Bhríde. Another influence on her singing was Áine bean Uí Ghallchóir, Annie John. Máire spent some years as a school teacher and is currently teaching in St Patrick's College, Drumcondra, Dublin. She performs at numerous festivals and organises singing workshops throughout Ireland and abroad.

Long ago there was a fellow called John Dunne, living at Tullyatten, and one night he was on his céilí in Peter Monaghan's of Corrabuggy and when he was going home he was crossing a field of Johnny Deignan's. And he saw a crowd of lads playing football. He walked on and took no interest in them. One of them gave the ball a kick and the ball struck his leg. It hit him so hard that he got lame, and he went home and never was able to walk again – he was a cripple for the rest of his life.

Told by Michael Gargan (60), Losset, Moybologue and Kilmainhamwood, to P.J. Gaynor in October, 1942. (NFC 832:469)

The account from the Cavan-Meath area indicates that even accidental involvement in, or experience of the fairy world, can result in a lasting negative affect in terms of the human being's life. Night-rambling is not without its dangers.

The Lutharadán's Jig

played on the fiddle by Junior Crehan

This jig is a composition of Junior Crehan (1908 -98), the fiddle and concertina player, singer, and storyteller from Bonavilla, Mullagh in west Clare. Music, storytelling and dancing were central to his life and Junior's knowledge of farming lore and local history was extraordinary. Many of Junior's compositions are now firmly established in the Irish traditional music repertoire. These include 'The Mist Covered Mountain', 'Farewell to Miltown Malbay', 'Poll an Mhadra Uisce' and 'Caisleán an Óir'. Tom Munnelly collected much music and lore from Junior and has catalogued this along with a detailed biographical account. (See Munnelly 1998 and 1999).

Junior often had a story to tell about the inspiration for his many tunes and this one came to him when he decided to try and catch one of the little people.

Fairies were part of Junior's life. He said he would contradict anyone who says fairies don't exist because as he said: 'I mixed in them since I was born'. In this account he tells of a time when he was about ten years married and things started to go badly. He noticed one morning that things around the fire were different to the way in which he had left them at night and so he decided to stay up and watch. He called one of his sons and they both hid behind a cupboard. And it wasn't long before they heard a scraping in the chimney and a small little man came down. He was the *lutharadán* or leprechaun. He arranged the embers and put down a little saucepan in the coals and stirred it. Junior ran and caught him and asked him for a crock of gold. The *lutharadán* had no gold to give him but gave him advice instead as to how he could become rich. 'Keep the brood mare, keep the sow in young, sow a small seed of the barley.'

The *lutharadán* saw Junior's fiddle hanging on the wall and asked him if he was a musician. Junior replied that he was and the *lutharadán* said:

'I'll give you a tune too,' says he, and he started to jig. And between the power of the music and the jigging, didn't myself and the lad fall asleep and when we woke he was gone.

But I had a bit of the tune but the young lad was quicker than me, and between the two of us, a couple of days after, hadn't we the tune. 'Twas a nice jig.'

The *luthradán* or *lurgadán* are among other names for the better-known leipreachán, a small supernatural man in Irish folklore. Hundreds of accounts and related legends are contained in the National Folklore Collection. The *leipreachán's* appearance is attested to throughout Ireland and he is generally unaccompanied when he makes himself known to a human being. Often, the human demands gold or information as to where gold is hidden but by means of trickery the *luthradán* or *leipreachán* escapes. (See Ó Giolláin, 1982, 1984)

Tom Munnelly's diary entry for this occasion includes the following account:

> Out yet again with Junior Crehan. Brought along a 1/2 doz. A good night's work. ….worked until midnight.

This man caught the leipreachán *one morning near Clais a'Naylor [Glaise Naylor] and made close prisoner of him. There was no chance that he would get off until he told the man where the gold was.*

'If you bring me out to the fort field, I'll show you where the gold is.'

The man brought him out and the fairy showed him a big buachalán. [ragwort]

'Dig under this weed tomorrow morning and you'll get a crock of gold.'

'Wait,' says he, 'and we'll mark it.'

The Otherworld *Music & Song from Irish Tradition*

Junior Crehan

'Take off my right garter and tie it round the buachalán *and you'll know where to dig in the morning.' The man did as he was told and let the little man go.*

When he came out in the morning there was a red garter on every buachalán *in the field, thousands of them, all the same size and the same pattern.*

Told by Michael Quirke (48), Moher West, Knockavilla Tipperary, 20.10.1937 (NFC 407:233).

Generally the *leipreachán* outwits the mortal. Otherworld beings, and especially the *leipreachán*, were often associated with giving good advice to human beings in all spheres of life. The belief in hidden treasure and assistance from supernatural beings in locating such treasure is prevalent in oral tradition. This is evidenced, for example, by the title 'Hidden Treasure' which was the first essay title suggested in the booklet published by the Irish Folklore Commission and distributed to the primary schools as part of the Schools' Manuscripts Collection in 1937.

The Otherworld Music & Song from Irish Tradition

Ivy growing on roof of thatched house photographed at night, County Kerry, 1998. The ivy-leaf was used to play music, was reputed to have medicinal properties and was also used in the dyeing of clothes.

Tom Munnelly

Ceann Boirne [Black Head]

lilted by Micho Russell

All she had when she came back was the old tune called 'Ceann Boirne'. But I couldn't play 'Ceann Boirne'. So, I could just lilt it for you the way that I heard [it]. This was all she had anyway when she came back.

Ceann Boirne, or Black Head, lies a few miles to the north of Doolin where Micho Russell lived all his life. Irish folk tradition abounds in tales and legends of mortals who were enticed by mysterious otherworldly music and went in search of that music. The humans were often missing for a time before re-emerging back to the real world. Micho introduced the legend and tune in the following manner:

Ceann Boirne – Black Head, you know… Well, this girl was bringing bread from a place called Ballyvaughan to a place called The Lodge in Murúch and when she was passing this place in Gleninagh beyond she heard music coming out from a lios, a kind of a fort, so, she went in to investigate to know what, where they were coming from. So, anyways, she was missing for three or four days and no one didn't know where she was.

The tune Micho lilts is a version of the popular west Clare jig, 'The Cliffs of Moher.'

Katrine Chang, from Denmark, made a trip to Ireland in 1993 and while here she made sound recordings and took photographs of musicians, singers and storytellers. Katrine donated a copy of her recordings of Micho to the National Folklore Collection.

Ceann Boirne – Black Head, County Clare, 2012.

The Otherworld Music & Song from Irish Tradition

*One day as an old man named Cormac
was crossing Garland's Hill, he heard
music near him. The music moved on to
the road and Cormac followed it. Soon
they had him dancing for the first time
in this life, and he danced until he wore
the soles of his boots. When they were
leaving, they all started to cheer and shout
'Bravo, Mac Cormac, Bravo, Mac Cormac'.
(NFCS 932: 104-105)*

The music of the Otherworld was so compelling
that people were drawn to it and drawn into the
dance. The account written by the teacher, Iníon
Nic Aodha, at Kednaminsha School, Inishkeen,
Donaghmoyne, County Monaghan in 1939
as part of the Schools' Manuscripts Collection
painted this phenomenon in a striking fashion.
Once again, the story is strengthened by the
inclusion of the location of the mysterious
happening and the naming of the old man. The
personal pronoun 'they' is used rather than risk
a direct reference to the fairies.

Amhrán an Phúca [The Song of the Pooka]

sung by Sarah Ghriallais

Bhí mise ag gabháil Gaillimh is ní bréag atá mé a rá libh,
Ní raibh mórán den lá ann is mé ag fágáil an tí,
Ach gabháil soir Loch an Iolra is ea a chonaic mé an scáile,
Bhí a leath deiridh in airde is é ar mhullach a chinn.

Ó theann mise isteach leis go ndearcfainn ní b'fhearr é,
Is go deimhin má theannas, ní theannfainn aríst.
Mar thosaigh sé ag corraí is ag lúbadh a chuid cnámha,
Is bhí leithead Chruach Phádraig de chnoc ar a dhroim.

Ba é an beathaíoch ba haite é dhá dtiocfaidh is dá dtáinig,
Bhí leithead dhá chopóig de chluas os a chionn,
Bhí féasóg chomh tiubh air is go ndéanfadh sí cábla,
Is gan trácht ar an bhfásach bhí ar mhullach a chinn.

Ó thosaigh sé ag pramsáil is ag léimneacht in airde,
Is chloisfeá chaon ráig uaidh go réidh in Áth Cinn.
Ach is mise bhí i dteannta is gan goir agam é a fhágáil,
Is gan fios agam cén t-am mbeadh an bás os mo chionn.

Bhí a dhá chois chomh fada le dhá mhaide rámha,
Is bhí leithead dhá bhráillín go maith ina dhroim,
Is bhí a chuid cluasa chomh leathan le copógaí sráide,
Bhí mallí chomh crochta air le buntsop an tí.

Nach mise bhí i dteannta is mé i mo staic i mbéal bearna,
Ag guí go cráifeach ag iarraidh theacht tríd,
Ach smaoiníos i m'intinn go ngéaróinn mo rásúr,
Is rinneas búistéireacht ghránna air ó dhrioball go droim.

Ó tharraing mé liom é is cheanglaíos den aill é,
Sa gcaoi nach mbeadh fáil air go dtiocfadh sé thríd,
Ach go deimhin má tharraingíos ní dheachaigh cónra ná clár air,
Is tá sé ar thóin an pholl báite is nár thaga sé aníos.

Tá cúpla amhrán greannmhar ar fáil faoin bpearsa neamhshaolta seo, pearsa atá sa traidisiún i dtíortha eile freisin. Bíonn cruthanna éagsúla ar an bpúca agus uaireanta is i gcló capaill a thagann sé i measc na ndaoine. In amanna, crochann sé an duine leis tríd an aer go dtí an saol eile. Cur síos atá san amhrán ag Sarah Ghriallais ar eachtra inar casadh an púca ar an bhfile agus ba ghránna an bheathach a bhí ann. D'éirigh leis an bhfile an púca a cheannsú.

Rinne an file Micheál Mhac Suibhne amhrán greannmhar a bhfuil an t-ainm céanna air (Ó Máille 1933) agus ar thaifeadaigh Vail Ó Flatharta leagan de don cheirnín 'Bláth na nAirní' ach de réir cosúlachta, níl aon leagan foilsithe den amhrán ag Sarah Ghriallais ar fáil. Rinne Deasún Breatnach dianstaidéar ar an bpúca sa traidisiún béil a foilsíodh i bhfoirm leabhair. (Breatnach 1993)

As Muicineach idir Dhá Sháile í Sorcha Bean Uí Chonghaile nó Sarah Ghriallais mar is fearr aithne uirthi. Ghnóthaigh sí Corn Uí Riada sa mbliain 1984. Chaith sí tamall de bhlianta ag obair i Sasana agus i Meiriceá. Tá cáil na fonnadóireachta ar a beirt deirfiúr, Neain agus Nóra, freisin. I measc an ábhair uaithi atá foilsithe tá dlúthdhiosca 'Sean-Nós du Connemara' (2001). Chuala sí 'Amhrán an Phúca' ó fhear as Gleann Mhac Muirinn, Tom Bhill nó Tomás Ó Céidigh. B'fhéidir go mba é Tom féin a rinne an t-amhrán mar go mbíodh sé á ndéanamh.

The Song of the Pooka

A few comic songs in Irish have been composed about this otherworldly creature the 'púca'. The creature, which is also known in other countries and traditions, sometimes as puck, takes different forms and often appears in the shape of a horse. It may carry a human away through the air to the Otherworld. The song Sarah Ghriallais sings here describes an occasion when the songmaker met with the 'púca' who was an ugly creature. The poet succeeded in overcoming the 'púca'. Deasún Breatnach has undertaken a detailed study of the 'púca' (Breatnach 1993).

Another light-hearted song also entitled 'Amhrán an Phúca' was composed by Micheál Mhac Suibhne (Ó Máille 1933) and recorded by Vail Ó Flatharta on the long-playing record *Bláth na nAirní*. No published version of Sarah's song has come to light, however.

I was going to Galway and I tell you no lie,
It was barely daybreak as I left the house,
But going east by Loch an Iolra
I saw the shadow,
Its end sticking upwards and it on
its head.

I drew closer to see it better,
And if I did, I wouldn't do the same again,
Because it started to shake and
bend its bones
And it had a lump as big as
Croagh Patrick on its back.

It was the strangest living thing that
could or ever did appear,
And its ears like two dock leaves stood
out from its head,
Its beard was so thick it would make a cable,
Not to mention the wild growth on
top of its head.

As it started to prance and jump up,
You would easily hear every roar
in Headford,
But I was caught and no chance to escape,
Not knowing when death would visit me.

Its two legs were as long as two oars,
And its back was easily the width
of two sheets,
Its ears were as wide as leaves of
the doc plant,
Its eyebrows hung just like the straw
thatch of the house.

I was caught and stuck in the gap
Praying fervently that I could come through,
But I thought in my mind I would sharpen
my razor,
And I tore it and cut it from its tail
to its back.

I dragged it with me and tied it at the cliff,
In a manner that meant it could
never be found.
It was crooked and misshapen and
could not fit in a coffin,
And it now lies on the sea bed and
may it never come up.

Sorcha Uí Chonghaile, better known as Sarah Ghriallais, is from Muicineach idir Dhá Sháile, County Galway. She won Corn Uí Riada at the Oireachtas Singing Competition in 1984. She spent some years working in England and in America and returned to Ireland in 1974. Her audio publications include the French issue *Sean-Nós du Connemara*, (2001). Sarah first heard the song 'Amhrán an Phúca' from a man from Gleann Mhac Muirinn, County Galway, 'Tom Bhill' or Tomás Ó Céidigh who may also have been the author as he is known to have made a number of other songs.

In County Carlow and generally in Leinster, as well as I know, the 'púca' is an enchanted horse, which lies on the grass as quiet as a lamb in some conspicuous spot until some unwary individual decided to go for a ride on him. God help him, who goes for a nocturnal ride on a 'púca'. Seven tours of the earth is nothing to him. Hell for leather the whole time and at the end of the joy ride he invariably flings off his victim into the middle of a brake of briars, nettles, etc.

An effigy known as 'The Púca's Head' figures on many of the old ruined castles. 'You were at the castle of Clonmore today? Did you see the púca's head?' And if you confess that you did not, say you saw nothing. If a man caught his horse, or a neighbour's horse after dusk no power on earth would persuade him to get up on it. And many a man wouldn't mount his own at night even if he saw him coming out of his own stable. Sure it might be the 'púca'.

Told by John English, Gort an Doire, Toom, County Limerick to P. Mac Domhnaill, 27.1.1938. (NFC 462:356)

The storyteller in the example above offers sympathy to anyone taken away on the enchanted horse - the 'púca' - for a night-time ride around the earth. The 'púca' is not seen in most instances as a benign figure and people were quite afraid of being carried off by this overly energetic horse with no idea of how, where or when they might return.

Muicineach idir Dhá Sháile, County Galway, 2011. The sea is on either side of this place in Conamara as indicated in the phrase 'idir dhá sháile'.

The Banshee

told by Edward Kendellan

Edward Kendellan:

I could tell you a banshee one – as a matter of fact if there is such a thing. I have heard it twice. If there is such a thing. I'm not saying there is.

John Newman:

Where did you hear it?

Edward Kendellan:

In the back yard. It's an unmerciful wail. You often heard of cats now would fight you know. Well, now, they're only in the shade. This wail I heard was unmerciful. But on each occasion there was a death in the one house in this terrace.

Edward Kendellan was a brush maker and a lorry driver. He was aged seventy-two and lived in Stoneybatter, Dublin when this recording was made in 1980, as part of the Urban Folklore Project, by collector John Newman. The Urban Folklore Project includes other recordings of Edward made by Éilís Ní Dhuibhne. Edward spoke of apprenticeship programmes, of making brooms and brushes and had tales of local characters.

John Newman spent around a year working with the Urban Folklore Project. Most of his collecting was done in the Grand Canal district and around Aughrim Street in Dublin.

Oh, Yes; I always heard them say that families when they're dying – You'll get other people saying: 'Aw, I heard the banshee.'

The Banshee follows certain families here. The Banshee follows the Kilduffs, and Kilorans and the Mullaneys.

Told by Joseph Meehan, Shranagh, Sooey, County Sligo to Michael J. Murphy in 1969. (NFC 1757:228)

Stoneybatter, Dublin, 1980.

The Otherworld Music & Song from Irish Tradition

139

The banshee is believed to have associations with certain families and surnames. Her cry is considered to be a portent of a death. (See Lysaght, 1985)

One morning Jack Leonard was cutting turf on Gilmore's bog when he saw a banshee coming towards him clapping her hands and crying, saying: 'A Mhuire, Mhuire, Mhuire.' He ran away shouting and into Gilmore's. 'I am done now,' said he, shouting, 'what'll I do at all?' 'Why?' said Mrs Gilmore, 'What is wrong with you?' 'Oh, I saw the banshee,' said he, 'I must be going to die.' Mrs Gilmore told him to stop his foolishness and not to be saying that he was going to die. Mrs Gilmore went outside with him and they could hear the crying. Mrs Gilmore said to Jack that it must be crying some of the McLoughlins for it seemed to be crying round their house. Next morning Mrs Gilmore got a letter from her sister in America who told in that letter that the day before she wrote she was at Mrs McLoughlin's funeral. Some say that a banshee is one of the dead person's friends, come to cry their own when they are dying. If you look behind you at a banshee she will throw her comb at you and poison you.

From Hannah Fitzsimons, Delvin, County Westmeath, 1977. (NFC 1890: 57)

John Newman

The Otherworld *Music & Song from Irish Tradition*

The Lilting Banshee and *An Rógaire Dubh* [*The Black Rogue*]

whistled by Robert Harvey

'The Lilting Banshee' is a jig, which appears to have common currency throughout the traditional music community. Other names for it include 'The Wailing Banshee', 'The Whistling Banshee', 'The Banshee's Lament' as well as more local titles such as 'The Moyasta Jig', 'The Sligo Jig' and the 'Killaloe Boat'.

Sometimes a mortal musician is said to have only one or two tunes before an encounter with the Otherworld and, often, where this occurs, the musician may be on his way to a wedding or a dance and is afraid he will be mocked because he will have to play the same tune or tunes throughout the entire evening. Occasionally, the name of the only tune known to the musician is the well-known and often played jig 'An Rógaire Dubh' ['The Black Rogue'].

'An Rógaire Dubh' has always been a popular tune among musicians and singers throughout Ireland. It is particularly associated with Conamara where it is almost a mandatory element of any accordion player's repertoire. Maggie McDonagh, the celebrated singer from the island of Fínis, Carna, County Galway has recorded words to this tune of which the first verse is:

Tá mo stocaí is mo bhróga ag an rógaire dubh,
Mo stocaí is mo bhróga ag an rógaire dubh,
Tá mo stocaí is mo bhróga ag an rógaire dubh,
Is mo naipcín póca bliain sa lá inniu.

The black scoundrel has my stockings and shoes,
The black scoundrel has my stockings and shoes,
The black scoundrel has my stockings and shoes,
And has my pocket-handkerchief for a year from today.

The writer, John Millington Synge (1871-1909) played the 'Black Rogue' on the fiddle during his stay in the Aran Islands and wrote that it is 'only when I play some jig like the 'Black Rogue' – which is known on the island - that they seem to respond to the full meaning of the notes' and also wrote when he played the same tune in Aran 'in a moment a tall man bounded out from his stool under the chimney and began flying round the kitchen with peculiarly sure and graceful bravado'. (Synge 2008, 179,181)

Writers and literary scholars have long been fascinated by the 'púca' and tales of otherworldly interventions. Douglas Hyde (Dubhghlas de hÍde) (1860-1949) was a scholar of Irish and a

The Piper and the Fairies

Long ago there lived over near Crossmolina, a simple half-witted fellow who had a set of pipes. He was fond of music, and the only tune that he was able to play was the "roguara dhu" (the black rogue), nor was he capable of learning any other tune. Being a fool more or less, people were continually humbugging him, giving him drink and bringing him to social parties, wedding feasts and dances &c. They used to praise him highly for his music and tell him his equal was not in Ireland, and the poor fool believed all their jesting, and the people derived great fun from him.

Extract from an account contributed by Michael Corduff, Erris, County Mayo in the late 1950s.

The Otherworld Music & Song from Irish Tradition

The Otherworld *Music & Song from Irish Tradition*

noted collector of folklore. He makes reference to the 'púca' in his *Leabhar Sgeulaigheachta*. The poet William Butler Yeats (1865-1939) offers a translation of Hyde's story which he calls 'The Piper and the Púca'. The translation first appeared in Yeats' *Fairy and Folk Tales of the Irish Peasantry* (1889). Hyde originally had the story from Máire Ní Bhairéad, Ballinrobe, County Galway:

Oíche Shamhna bhí an píobaire ag teacht abhaile ó theach damhsa, agus é leath ar meisce. Nuair tháinig sé go droichead beag in aice le teach a mháthar d'fháisc sé na píobaí air, agus thoisigh sé ag seinm an Rógaire Dubh.

Tháinig an Púca taobh thiar de agus chaith sé ar a dhroim féin é. Bhí adharca fada ar an bPúca agus fuair an Píobaire greim daingean orthu. Ansin dúirt sé: 'Léirscrios ort! A bheithigh ghránna, lig abhaile mé, tá píosa deich bpinne agam do mo mháthair, agus tá oireasa snisín uirthi.'

'Ná bac le do mháthair,' arsa an Púca, 'ach coinnigh do ghreim, má thitfidh tú brisfidh tú do mhuinéal agus do phíobaí.'

Ansin dúirt an Púca leis: 'séid suas dom an tSeanbhean Bhocht.'

'Níl eolas agam air,' arsa an Píobaire

'Ná bac le d'eolas,' arsa an Púca, 'séid suas agus béarfaidh mise eolas duit.'

Do chuir an píobaire gaoth ina mhála agus sheinn sé ceol do chuir iontas air féin.

(see De h-Íde 1899, 96-97)

One night the piper was coming home from a house where there had been a dance, and he half drunk. When he came to a little bridge that was up by his mother's house, he squeezed the pipes on, and began playing the "Black Rogue" (an rógaire dubh). The Púca came behind him and flung him up on his own back. There were long horns on the Púca, and the pipers got a good grip of them, and then he said –

"Destruction on you, you nasty beast, let me home. I have a ten-penny piece in my pocket for my mother and she wants snuff."

"Never mind your mother," said the Púca, "but keep your hold. If you fall, you will break your neck and your pipes." Then the Púca said to him "Play up for me the 'Shan Van Vocht' (an t-seann-bhean bhocht)."

"I don't know it," said the piper.

"Never mind whether you do or you don't," said the Púca. "Play up, and I'll make you know."

The piper put wind in his bag, and he played such music as made himself wonder.

(Yeats 1888)

Robert Harvey, from Roundwood, Mountrath, County Laois, is a graduate of music education from Trinity College Dublin. He won the All-Ireland Whistling competition five times in a row, from 2002 to 2006. Robert is also an accomplished flute and tin-whistle player.

An Cailín Deas Rua [The Nice Red-Haired Girl]

sung by Nell Ní Chróinín

In aisling dom féin aréir is mé im' leabaidh trím shuan,
Go rabhasa le pósadh lem' stór chroí go hintinneach suairc.
Bhí rince agus ceol go leor á scaipeadh lem' chluais,
Agus céad ghiní óir im' chóir ag mo chailín deas rua.

Is é Tiobraid Árann a fhágas ar maidin Dé Luain,
Níor stadas den stair sin go dtánaig go Corcaigh na gcuan,
Cé gheobhainn os cionn cláir ann ach mo ghrá is í ag imirt ar scuaib,
Is ar iompó an mhámha bhí an cíoná ag an gcailín deas rua.

Siúd ort a Sheáin mar ní fhágfam an baile go Luan,
Is go bhfuil mo chroí cráite gan fáil ar an 'toddy' ná a luach,
Is gurb é deir na mná óga mb'fhearr leo mé marbh san uaigh,
Mura thréigfeadsa an chlár, an chart is an cailín deas rua.

Ní thréigfeadsa an clár an chairt ná an cnagairt cruaidh.
Ní thréigfear ná Máire an bhean mhánla is í ainnir na gcuach.
Ar aonach an Mhárta thugas grá agus taitneamh dá grua,
Is a rún cheart mo chléibh ná tréig mé mar gheall ar na buaibh.

Léan ar na buaibh is buartha a fhágaid siad mná.
Bíonn braon ar a ngrua ón Luan go dtí maidin Dé Máirt.
A liacht cailín chiúin stuama, nár dhual dóibh imeacht chun fáin,
Agus leibidí luatha fáil buacais is gradam ina n-áit.

Do chonacsa í inné in éadach siopa i bhfad uaim,
Ba bhreátha í ná Venus an spéirbhean, is í ainnir na gcuach.
Níl aon gheallúint sa tsaol ón spéir go dtí an dtalamh anuas,
Nár thug sí dom féin is ina dhiaidh sin d'imigh sí uaim.

Níl aon tslat insan choill ná fuil snaidhm ina bun nó ina barr,
Níl aon bhreac ins an linn ná héiríonn ar bharr uisce ag snámh,
Níl aon sagart sa ríocht ná héiríonn chun Aifreann a rá,
Ach ó d'imigh sí uaim ní móide go mbraithim an lá.

The Otherworld *Music & Song from Irish Tradition*

Bhí rath agus beocht ar leith ag roinnt leis an aisling sa 17ú agus san 18ú aois agus ba iad filí agus scríbhneoirí chúige Mumhan ba mhó a chum na haislingí. Sna hamhráin agus sna dánta seo is iondúil go dtagann spéirbhean, arb í Éire atá i gceist in amanna, i láthair an fhile. Uaireanta, déanann sí gearán faoi na hathruithe polaitiúla atá i réim in Éirinn nó faoin bhfulaingt ag an uasal aicme Gaelach a bhfuil a stádas agus a cumhacht caillte aici. Is iomaí aisling ghrá ann chomh maith leis an aisling fháithchiallach agus is sampla den chineál sin aislinge é 'An Cailín Deas Rua'. San aisling seo samhlaíonn an file go bhfuil sé lena ghrá-geal a phósadh. Ach faigheann sé amach ansin go bhfuil sé tréigthe aici.

Rugadh agus tógadh Nell Ní Chróinín i mBéal Átha an Ghaorthaidh, i nGaeltacht Mhúscraí. Bhí amhránaíocht agus ceol mórthimpeall uirthi i gcónaí agus í ag fás aníos agus ní haon ionadh mar sin go raibh suim aici i gcúrsaí ceoil ina hóige. Tar éis bhás Dhiarmuidín Mhaidhcí Uí Shúilleabháin bunaíodh scéim amhránaíochta Aisling Gheal chun ranganna amhránaíochta a chur ar fáil do dhaoine óga ar fud an cheantair ar mhaithe leis na hamhráin áitiúla a scaipeadh agus a chaomhnú. Thosaigh Nell ag freastal ar ranganna amhránaíochta le Máire Ní Chéilleachair nuair a bhí sí deich mbliana d'aois agus tá sí ag canadh ó shin i leith, agus baineann sí fíor-thaitneamh as. Fuair sí cuid mhaith dá hamhráin ó Eoiní Maidhcí Ó Súilleabháin agus Eibhlís Ní Shúilleabháin. Chuala Nell taifeadadh d'Iarla Ó Lionáird ag rá an amhráin seo agus fuair sí na focail ó Mháirín Maidhcí Ní Shúilleabháin.

Nell Ní Chróinín.

The Nice Red-Haired Girl

'Aisling' or vision poetry flourished during the 17th and 18th centuries and has a special association with the poets and writers of Munster. In these poems and songs, a beautiful woman, who is sometimes Ireland personified, appears to the poet. The woman often laments the changed political circumstances that now prevail or complains of the loss of power and prestige endured by the Irish ruling political classes and their retinue of poets and writers. Along with political allegory, songs of love occur in 'aisling' form. In this particular example 'An Cailín Deas Rua' ('The Nice Red-Haired Girl') the loved one appears to the poet at night. In the vision, the poet imagines he will marry her but then discovers that she has abandoned him.

A vision last night came to me as
I lay in my bed,
My spirits they soared as I was
to be married.
Sweet music and dance filled up my head,
And a hundred gold guineas my nice
red-haired girl brought to me.

I left Tipperary on a Monday morning,
And made no stop until I reached
Cork harbour.
Who should I find there but my love and
she winning at cards,
And when the trump card was turned
it was the red-haired girl was winning.

Come along Seán because I won't
leave home until Sunday,
And I am heartworn and troubled as
I can't find the price of a drink,
And the young girls say they'd rather
me dead and in my grave,
Than gambling and drinking and
loving the nice red-haired girl.

I'll not give up the boards, card and drink,
And I'll not give up Máire the gracious
woman with the flowing hair,
At the fair in March I gave her love
and affection,
And my true love, do not abandon me
for the sake of possessions.

My curse on the cattle because their lure causes tears,
With girls' cheeks wet from Monday until Tuesday morning,
Many a steady, wise girl would not have been led,
Not following their heart and chasing status instead.

Yesterday, I saw her from a distance and she dressed all fine,
Lovelier than Venus, a vision with flowing hair.
She promised me everything between earth and sky,
But after that, she left me.

There is not a branch in the wood that is not twisted or gnarled,
No fish in the pond that doesn't rise to the top.
There is not a priest in the kingdom that doesn't rise to say Mass,
But since she left I can hardly sense the day.

Nell Ní Chróinín was born and grew up in Béal Átha an Ghaorthaidh, in the Irish-speaking district of Múscraí, County Cork. She was surrounded by singing and music as a child. Following the death of the noted local singer, Diarmuidín Maidhcí Ó Súilleabháin, a scheme 'Aisling Gheal' was established to provide singing classes for young people to disseminate and preserve local songs. Nell began attending singing classes with Máire Ní Chéilleachair when she was ten years old. She has been singing ever since and enjoys it immensely. She got many of her songs from Eoiní Maidhcí Ó Súilleabháin and Eibhlís Ní Shúilleabháin. Nell heard a recording of this particular song from Iarla Ó Lionáird and she got the words from Máirín Mhaidhcí Shúilleabháin.

Flag bridge across the Lee, Béal Átha an Ghaorthaidh, County Cork, c. 1924.

Ar bhruach na Laoi san oíche casadh mé,
Gan bhuairt ar m'aigne ba dhóigh
liom féin,
Go ndeachas fad slí le díth mo mhearathail,
I gcuantaibh daingne nárbh fhearr dom é,
Do shuíos-sa síos go diach gan eagla,
Faoi ard-tor draighin go fíortha ceartaithe,
Do dhearcas lem thaoibh an rí-bhean
mhaisiúil,
Gan súil le casadh go ruig fainne an lae.

Roibeard Muiris (90), Leathanach, Drom Dá
Liag, Contae Chorcaí a thug do Sheán Ó Briain,
24.7.1934. Chuala Roibeard é in 1874 ó
Dhonncha Ó Drisceoil. (CBÉ 46:354)

One night as I was by the banks of the Lee,
Without a care in the world, I thought,
Until I went astray with dizziness,
In closed recesses which did not
benefit me.
I sat down without fear,
Under a tall, shapely, thorn-bush
I saw beside me a beautiful,
noble woman,
And I hoped she would not leave
until break of day.

Given by Roibeard Muirls (90),
Leathanach, Drom Dá Liag,
County Cork to Seán Ó Briain, 24.7.1934.
Roibeard heard it in 1874 from
Donncha Ó Drisceoil. (CBÉ 46:354)

A mystical encounter takes place on the banks of the river Lee. Most rivers in Ireland have feminine names and are frequently associated with a goddess. Typical of 'aisling' or vision poetry is the concept of parting at daybreak as the poet and the idealised woman go their separate ways.

James Martin was born in Lough Crew, County Meath in the nineteenth century. He was the son of poor parents. Consequently he never received any education because it was harder for poor people to educate their children at that time than at the present. One night when Martin was grown up he dreamt that if he would go to a fort at midnight on a certain night he would get his fortune. Martin dreamt the same thing three nights in succession. But if he went he would lose some part of his body. Martin went to the fort on the night named and he saw a fiddle, a poet book and pen and ink. He had his choice of either, so he took up the book of poems. When he did so, the pen jumped out of the ink bottle and knocked out his eye, so from that day forth Martin had only one eye, but he could read and compose poems and his name spread over the county of Meath for his wisdom. Martin died in the nineteenth century and was buried at Moylough, County Meath.

Told by Dan Kelly, Baltrasna, Oldcastle, County Meath to Eithne Kearney, 1937-1939. (NFCS 716:276)

The belief in dreams as portents of good or bad fortune is well-attested. The magic power of three and the significant hour of midnight feature here. A possible interpretation of the narrative is that the poetic powers and fame granted to James Martin come at a price.

Paddy Bán Quigley told by John Doherty
and
The Boys of Malin Head played on the fiddle by John Doherty

Paddy Glackin:

John, I've often heard, heard it said from my own father and I've heard it from other musicians around that the wee people have a lot to do with the music?

John Doherty:

They have surely. Oh, they have surely. There's one thing I do know that the creatures, that they were heard playing. Oh, indeed they were heard playing and there was a piper, one time his name was Quigley and he played the pipes everywhere from Glenfin to Gleann Colm Cille, from there to the Rosses and, and I think up this far. They called him Paddy Bán, Paddy Bán Quigley. Ah, he was a good piper. But in any case, the poor soul, he was invited to play in Ballinamore, near Brockagh or away beyond Glenties. He was invited for to play there at a party and, oh God it was a party that was to be in Ballinamore, but in any case he was a proud kind of a man, he had a proud notion and it was all walking that time, there was no cars, there were no cars and it was all walking. But he walked on 'til he went to Glenties and there was a woman living in Glenties, she run a sort of a café there and he thought he would go in and have his dinner. And she just spoke freely to him, you know that he would have to take his time 'til those other people would be served. And ... what do you think, didn't he take a huff and he walked out and he wouldn't halt and he had then about ten miles to go to Ballinamore. And he walked it all along and when he went as far as a place they called Shelligan, Shelligan school, the poor soul. He gave up there. He took what they call, they call it in Irish *féar gorta*, that's a hunger weakness. He took that hunger weakness and he died there. Ah, the poor soul, he was got then, he was dead. He used to go in to Gleann Colm Cille for to play, to play for the people in there on the pipes, he used to go in as far as a place they call Malinbeg. The people knew

him very well but in any case the fishermen there would go on out to sea a bit out from the big cliffs you know to fish.

And some time after Paddy Bán Quigley died, the men were out on a, on a wee boat, three men, and just there the piper began just up on the face of the spink or cliff as I would call it, and one man called up in Irish, 'twas all Irish was going: *'Cé - cé atá ag seinm ansin?'* And the word answered back: *'Tá mise, Paddy Bán Quigley.'* And the man dead. A cliff of nine hundred feet. Nobody could stand there or be there. And so, the men got so very much afraid that they turned the boat and that they come back home. And 'twas the man's voice, surely, the dead man's voice. Aye, Paddy Bán Quigley. Oh, he was a splendid piper.

The fiddle player John Doherty told Paddy Glackin that he had this tune of Paddy Bán Quigley's saying it was 'old, an old reel of Paddy Bán Quigley's that he played on the pipes. It's played in the pipe style, you know. In his style, but it is just one old reel, that's all I know'.

Irish oral tradition is rich in accounts of the *féar gorta* or the hungry grass, a phenomenon believed by some to be related to times of famine, where an all-powerful hunger and accompanying weakness overcome a person as they are walking over a spot where a famine victim lies buried. Others believe that it occurs where fairy or otherworldly activity is taking place or has already taken place and it is sometimes said that if they did not have immediate access to food, people died at these particular spots.

John Doherty was a well-known travelling fiddle player (c.1895-1980). He came from a musical family. He was a craftsman and made tin fiddles. A number of recordings of his music have been published. He was a brother of Mickey Doherty who was also a well-known fiddle player.

This recording was made by Harry Bradshaw on the 20th of July, 1979. John was being interviewed by fiddle player Paddy Glackin for RTÉ in The Rock, Ballyshannon, County Donegal. It may be the last recording of John Doherty made before his death in 1980.

———

Cheannaigh mé caoirigh as a Chionn Gharbh agus d'imigh siad uaim agus d'imigh mé féin aon mhaidin amháin go hiontach luath dá gcuardú agus tháinig féar gorta orm agus tháinig mé anuas ag claí ann ag baint taca as an chlaí go dtáinig mé isteach i dteach a bhí ann, cóngarach ag an bhealach mhór. Tháinig mé isteach i dteach bheag nach raibh ann ach cailleach.

'By gorrah,' arsa mise. 'Tá féar gorta orm. Tá mé chóir a bheith caillte leis an ocras - chan fhuil dadaí réidh agat?'

'Níl,' ar sise, 'Tá pota preátaí ar an tine ach seo giota beag do arán preátaí. Bí dá chagnadh sin go dtaomfaidh mé na preátaí.' Agus sin an rud a bhí milis agamsa. Thaoim sí na preátaí agus chuir sí a cos suas ar a stól agus ní raibh a fhios agam in Éirinn cén uthbhairt a bhí uirthi. Goidé bhí uirthi ach cos mhaide agus scaoil sí an chos ag an ghlún agus chimil sí naprún de mhála saic a bhí uirthi thart cúl an 'heat' fán chois agus thoisigh agus bhrúigh na preátaí leis an chois agus

gan a fhios agamsa goidé bhí ar an chois sin. Sháith sí an maide briste isteach sa tine ansin go dtí go raibh sé dearg. Bhí craiceann mór de mhada bhreac in airde ar an bhalla. Leag sí an craiceann.

'Seo an áit a mbíonn an t-im ann nó ní thiocfadh liom a shábháil ar na cait.' Dar liom féin goidé mar íosfas mé sin agus an t-ocras mór. Thug sí léi an craiceann os cionn an phota agus sháith sí an maide briste faoi ruball an mhada agus thoisigh an t-im ag teacht ina sruth.

'"Come" anois, a chailleach', ar sise, 'ith do sháith.'

Leoga féin ní raibh mórán fonn orm é a ithe. Bhí mé féin ag sceathrach agus ag piocadh ribe ach d'ith mé oiread agus choinnigh beo mé. Rinne sí deoch bheag tae ansin agus ní raibh greim arán aici. Rinne sí a dícheall agus bhí mé féin i riocht cur amach go dtáinig mé fhad le teach an 'licence'. Fuair mé 'naggin' den chuid ab fhearr agus théigh mé suas agus ní raibh a dhath orm.

Neddy Moy (82), An Ghlaiseach Bheag, Cill Taobhóg, Contae Dhún na nGall a d'inis do Liam Mac Meanman, 23.20.1935. Chuala Neddy ó Condy Mhac Cormaic é in 1885 nuair a bhí Condy os cionn 85 bliana d'aois. (CBÉ 169:546-547)

John Doherty

I bought sheep from Cionn Garbh and they strayed and I went very early one morning in search of them and the 'hungry grass' came over me and I came down by a fence leaning on it for support until I came into a house near the road. I went into the little house where there was no one but an old woman.

'By gorrah,' I said. 'I have the 'hungry grass'. I am nearly dead with the hunger – have you any food prepared?'

'No,' she said, 'There is a pot of potatoes cooking on the fire here and all I have is a small piece of potato bread. Chew that until I strain the potatoes'. And that tasted very sweet to me. She strained the potatoes and she put her foot on a stool and I had no earthly idea what she was doing. She had a wooden leg and she released the leg at the knee and wiped her apron on a sack cloth that she was wearing, once around the leg, and she began to pound the potatoes with her leg and I did not know what was the matter with that leg. She stuck the broken stick into the fire then until it was reddened. There was the great skin of a brindled dog on the wall and she took the skin.

'That is where the butter is kept as I couldn't keep it safe from the cats.' I

thought to myself, how will I eat that and I am so hungry. She took the skin and placed it over the pot and she stuck the broken stick under the dog's tail and the butter began to flow.

'Come now, my dear,' she said, 'eat your fill.'

I was reluctant to eat it. I was separating and picking hair but I ate enough to keep me alive. She made a small drink of tea then and she didn't have a bite of bread. She did her best but I almost vomited until I came as far as the licensed house. I got a naggin of the best there and I heated it up and there wasn't a thing wrong with me.

Told by Neddy Moy (82), An Ghlaiseach Bheag, Cill Taobhóg, County Donegal to Liam Mac Meanman, 23.20.1935. Neddy heard it from Condy Mhac Cormaic in 1885 when Condy was more than 85 years old. (NFC 169:546-547)

Traditional cures often take apparently repellent forms. This arguably renders the cure more dramatic.

Bridgie Moroney and Lizzie Flanagan were stopping at Pateen Regan's house this night, and the two went to sleep in this room for themselves. In the middle of the night they heard the door opening and in walks the woman that was dead before they were born and she walks over to the milk-tub that was in the corner, and she takes a cupful of milk out of the tub and drinks it. Strange things used happen in his house.

Told by Séamus Ó Ceallaigh (47), Killeen, Beagh, County Galway to Seán Ó Flannagáin, 5.10.1937. (NFC 405:24)

This is a simple tale of a ghostly appearance from Galway. Stories of strange happenings and of ghosts are legion.

Paddy Glackin

The Otherworld *Music & Song from Irish Tradition*

Seán Ó Laoi and family,
An Cheathrú Rua, County Galway.   150

Recording sources

Cd 1

1. National Folklore Collection: NFC.Tom Munnelly, TM 38/B/6. NFC 2219: 59-60, 1972.

2. NFC Caoimhín Ó Danachair and Seán Ó hEochaidh, Disc 817, 1949. .

3. NFC Ríonach uí Ógáin, RÓ, 2007.

4. NFC TM 325/A/2 Interim vol.15: 130-131, 1974.

5. Harry Bradshaw, 1990.

6. Vocalion, 1922.

7. NFC TM 175/3, 1973.

8. NFC M52d Caoimhín Ó Danachair, 1948.

9. NFC RÓ, 2007.

10. NFC RÓ, 2008.

11. NFC Séamus Ennis 1945.

12. Peadar Ó Ceannabháin, 2008.

13. NFC Bróna Nic Amhlaoibh, UFP T0253(i), 1979.

14. NFC TM 361/B/6, 1976.

15. Saileog Ní Cheannabháin, 2008.

16. NFC TM 173/3. NFC 2227:123-124, 1973.

17. NFC Leo Corduff, T0217g, 1963.

18. RTÉ Radio Éireann, 1958.

19. Ciarán Ó Gealbháin, 2009.

20. NFC Micheál Ó Domhnaill T 22b/1, 1974.

21. Rónán Galvin, 2007.

Cd 2

1. Cormac Cannon, 2010.

2. NFC Caoimhín Ó Danachair and Seán Ó hEochaidh, Disc 853, 1949.

3. NFC Micheál Ó Domhnaill T 11/ T0025, 1974.

4. NFC TM 155/4. NFC 2227:36-37, 1973.

5. Tara Diamond, 2009.

6. NFC RÓ, 2008.

7. NFC RÓ, 2007.

8. NFC RÓ T15C, 1986.

9. NFC RÓ, 2007.

10. NFC Ciarán Bairéad, T053, 1958.

11. NFC RÓ 089,1986.

12. NFC RÓ, 2008.

13. NFC TM 637/8-9,1976. *Ciarán Mac Mathúna introduces music form Clare and Kerry* [2 cassettes] RTÉ, 1987.

14. Katrine Chang, 1992.

16. Sarah Ghriallais, 2008.

17. NFC John Newman UFP 0262(i), 1980.

18. NFC RÓ, 2007.

19. NFC RÓ, 2010.

20. RTÉ Harry Bradshaw, 1979.

Lone Tree, The Burren,
County Clare.

Additional information

Almqvist, B., 'Of Mermaids and marriages. Seamus Heaney's "Maighdean Mara" and Nuala Ní Dhomhnaill's "An Mhaighdean Mhara" in the Light of Folk Tradition', in *Béaloideas* (1990), 1-74.

'The Mélusine Legend in the Context of Irish Folk Tradition', in *Béaloideas* (1999), 13-69.

Beauty an Oileáin (CC56CD) Dublin 1992.

Bláth na nAirní.Vail Ó Flatharta Sings Traditional Songs from Connemara (CC45), Dublin 1987.

Bourke, A., *et al.*, (eds), *The Field Day Anthology of Irish Writing*, Vols. IV and V Irish Women's Writing and Traditions, Cork 2002.

Breathnach, B., *Ceol Rince na hÉireann 1*, Baile Átha Cliath 1963, 159.

Breatnach, D., *Chugat an Púca*, Baile Átha Cliath, 1993.

Buchan, D., 'The Legend of the Lughnasa Musician in Lowland Britain' in *Scottish Studies* (1979), 15-37.

Child, F.J. (ed.), *The English and Scottish Popular Ballads*, Boston 1882-98.

Collinson, F., *The Traditional and National Music of Scotland*, London 1966.

De h-Íde, D., *Leabhar Sgeulaigheachta*, Baile Átha Cliath 1889.

Donnelly, S., *The Early History of Piping in Ireland*, Dublin and Glasgow 2001.

Flower, R., *The Western Island or The Great Blasket*, Oxford 1944.

Hillers, B., 'Music from the Otherworld: Modern Gaelic Legends about Fairy Music', in *Proceedings of the Harvard Celtic Colloquium 14*, Boston 1997, 58-75.

Hughes, H., 'The Fairy Reel', in *Irish Folk Song Society Journal* vol. 1, London 1904, 19.

Huntington, G., Herrmann, L. and Moulden, J. (revised), *Sam Henry's Songs of the People*, Athens and London 1990.

Joyce, P.W, *Irish Music and Song*, Dublin 1903.

Laws, G. Malcolm, *American Balladry from British Broadsides*, Philadelphia 1957.

Lysaght, P., *The Banshee: a study in beliefs and legends about the Irish supernatural death-messenger*, Dublin 1985.

Mac Aoidh, C., *Between the Jigs and the Reels*, Leitrim 1994.

Mac Cárthaigh, C., 'The Ship-sinking Witch. A maritime folk legend from north-west Europe' in *Béaloideas* (1992-1993), 267-286.

Mac Cathmhaoil, S., 'Story of The Fairy Reel' in *Irish Folk Song Society Journal* vol. 1, London 1904, 19-21.

Mac Con Iomaire, L., 'Deora Aille – Máire Áine Ní Dhonnchadha agus a Cuid Amhrán', in *Léachtaí Cholm Cille 29* (1999) 7 – 36.

McGill, P., 'Notes and Queries – The Bruckless Drowning' in *The Donegal Annual*, vol. viii, no. 1 (1969), 116-117.

McGinley, T.C. (Kinnfaela), The Cliff Scenery of *South-Western Donegal* (1867), Donegal 2000.

Mac Neill, M., *The Festival of Lughnasa*, London 1962 (Dublin 1982, 2008).

Mac Seáin, S. (eag.), *Pléaráca Dhún Dealgan (Humours of Dundalk)*, Dundalk 1981 (1985).

Michael Coleman 1891-1945 (CEFCD 161) Dublin 1992.

Mitchell, P., *The Dance Music of Willie Clancy*, Dublin and Cork, 1976.

Munnelly, T., '"They're all the same!" Supernatural elements in narrative songs in the English language in Ireland' in *Béaloideas* (1992-1993), 173-196.

The Mount Callan Garland: Songs from the Repertoire of Tom Lenihan of Knockbrack, Miltown Malbay, Co. Clare, Dublin 1994.

'Junior Crehan of Bonnavilla in *Béaloideas* (1998), 59-161.

'Junior Crehan of Bonnavilla (Part 2) in *Béaloideas* (1999), 71-124.

Ó Catháin, S., 'The Robbers and the Captive Girl' in *Béaloideas* (1994), 109-146.

Ó Cearbhaill, P., 'An Púca i Logainmneacha' in *Ainm ii* (1987), 96-113.

O'Connor, A., *Child Murderess and Dead Child Traditions* FF Communications 249, Helsinki 1991.

The Blessed and the Damned: Sinful Women and Unbaptised Children in Irish Folklore, Oxford *et al.* 2005.

O'Daly, J., *The Poets and Poetry of Munster*, Dublin 1850.

Ó Gealbháin, C., 'Stair is Seanchas san Amhrán "Pilib Séimh Ó Fathaigh"'in *An Linn Bhuí: Iris Ghaeltacht na nDéise* (2006), 151-166.

Ó Giolláin, D., 'An Leipreachán san Ainmníocht' in *Béaloideas* (1982), 126-150.

'The Leipreachán and Fairies, Dwarfs and the Household Familiar: a comparative study' in *Béaloideas* (1984), 75-150.

'The Fairy Belief and Official Religion in Ireland' in Peter Narváez (ed.), *The Good People. New Fairylore Essays*, New York and London 1991, 199-214.

Ó hEochaidh, S., 'Seanchas Iascaireachta' in *Béaloideas* 1965 [1967], 52-53.

Ó hEochaidh, S., Ní Néill, M., Ó Catháin, S., *Síscéalta ó Thír Chonaill/ Fairy Legends from Donegal*, Baile Átha Cliath 1977.

Ó hÓgáin, D., *The Lore of Ireland*, Cork 2006.

Ó Máille, T., *Micheál Mhac Suibhne agus Filidh an tSléibhe*, Baile Átha Cliath 1933.

Ó Madagáin, B., 'Echoes of Magic in the Gaelic Song Tradition' in *Celtic Languages and Celtic Peoples*, Halifax 1992, 125-140.

Ó Muirgheasa, É., *Céad de Cheoltaibh Uladh*, Baile Átha Cliath 1915.

O'Neill, F., *The Dance Music of Ireland 1001 Gems*, Chicago 1907.

Irish Minstrels and Musicians, Chicago 1913.

Ó Súilleabháin, S. and Christiansen, Reidar Th., *The Types of the Irish Folktale*, FF Communications 188, Helsinki 1963.

Radner, J., *Feminist Messages: Coding in Women's Folk Culture*, Urbana and Chicago 1993.

Séamus Ennis. Ceol, Scéalta agus Amhráin, (CEFCD009) Dublin 2006 (1961).

Shields, H. 'The Dead Lover's Return in Modern English Ballad Tradition', in *Jahrbuch für Volksliedforschung*, Berlin 1972, 98 – 114.

Narrative Singing in Ireland, Dublin 1993.

Sorcha - Amhráin Shorcha Ní Ghuairim: Traditional Songs from Conamara (CEFCD 182) Dublin 2002.

Synge, J., *The Aran Islands*, London 2008 (Dublin/London 1907).

The Gravel Walks: The Fiddle Music of Mickey Doherty (CBÉ 002), Dublin 1990.

Thompson, S., *Motif-Index of Folk-Literature*, Copenhagen 1955-1958.

Ua Gallchobhair, S., 'Báthadh Phrochlaisc, The Bruckless Drownings on February 8th 1913', 2004 (unpublished).

uí Ógáin, R., and O'Connor, A., 'Spor ar an gCois agus gan an Chois ann: A study of "The Dead Lover's Return" in Irish Tradition', in *Béaloideas* (1983), 126 – 144.

uí Ógáin, R 'Music Learned from the Fairies', in *Béaloideas* (1992-1993), 197 – 214.

uí Ógáin, R. and Munnelly, T., 'The Song Tradition', in *The Field Day Anthology of Irish Writing*, vol. 4, Cork 2002.

Uther, H-J., *The Types of International Folktales*, FF Communcations 284-286, Helsinki 2004.

Wagner, H., *Gaeilge Theilinn*, Dublin 1959.

Yeats, W.B., *Fairy and Folk Tales of Ireland*, Gerrards Cross 1973 (*Fairy and Folk Tales of the Irish Peasantry* 1888).

http://library.efdss.org/archives accessed January 2012.

St John's Eve bonfire Co. Mayo.
The celebration of midsummer is
a widespread European tradition.

Photo credits:

The Otherworld *Music & Song from Irish Tradition*

The Otherworld Music & Song from Irish Tradition